BEYOND MENTORING

Comprehensive Induction Programs

How to attract, support, and retain new teachers

SECOND EDITION

Jon Saphier
Susan Freedman
Barbara Aschheim

*TEACHERS*²¹
34 Washington Street, Suite 220, Wellesley, MA 02481   781/416-0980   TEACHERS21.ORG

TABLE OF CONTENTS

TABLE OF CONTENTS

TABLE OF CONTENTS

Preface

Modification of an African proverb:
It takes a whole district to raise good teachers.

Five years ago we wrote the first edition of *Beyond Mentoring* to share our successful experience with a comprehensive induction program for new teachers. The model that guides this program has continued to support new teachers and to strengthen schools as professional learning communities. *Beyond Mentoring* is being used as a valuable guide in every state in the United States, in many countries, and on most of the continents.

With five additional years of experience and feedback from an increasingly diverse community of practitioners, we have updated the original *Beyond Mentoring* and added suggestions and strategies for using induction programs to strengthen the school as a professional learning community. This edition sets forth a vision and model for the comprehensive induction of beginning teachers that is implemented by Teachers[21] in its consulting work with teachers and administrators in urban, suburban, and rural school districts.

Beginning teachers do not start out proficient. They are novices, no matter how mature they are personally or how rigorous their academic background. Nor should we expect anything else. We do have a right to expect that they emerge from their preparation programs with deep content knowledge of their subjects. Unfortunately, there is ample reason to doubt that, in many cases, they do have this knowledge.

At the same time, there is an array of proficiencies we would be foolish to assume and presumptuous to expect. Most beginning teachers do not know how to set expectations, shape interpersonal climate, and teach routines during the opening days of school. How could they, never having had responsibility for doing so? In most cases, they have not been in classrooms during the first days or weeks of school, despite their student teaching or intern experiences.

Furthermore, they do not know how to manage the complexities of movement and flow in classrooms that are designed for active learning.

• They do not know how to differentiate instruction for students with different learning styles.

• They do not know how to respond to disruptive students or parent complaints.

• They do not know what is expected of them on back-to-school nights or in parent conferences.

• They do not know how to motivate low performing students who doubt their own abilities and believe they are incapable of meeting high standards.

• They do not know how to interact as a professional learner in a community of learners.

None of the above is criticism of beginning teachers or the institutions that prepare them. Novices are not supposed to know all the complexities of their craft at the beginning. It is, however, our responsibility to them and to the children they serve to provide them in their early years with the conditions for learning and reflection that support them as they engage in the complex practice of teaching. We need to provide them with a comprehensive array of supports that ensure that they will be successful and that the children in their classrooms will have an optimal opportunity to learn.

A comprehensive induction program involves more than just mentors. In fact, mentors alone, though a critical part of good induction, cannot be expected to provide the range of input, feedback, and support that beginning teachers need. Well-designed induction programs include specific roles for principals, superintendents, central office personnel, the teachers union, parents, school boards, and particularly the other staff members in the school or department where the beginning teacher works.

Nothing is more important to the learning of students than what their teachers know, believe, and can do. The pivotal importance of teachers to student achievement has been well documented (Marzano, 2001). What has been absent in the career paths of American teachers is the recognition that their work is intellectually complex, difficult, and demanding on a par with other developed professions - law, architecture, medicine. We do not provide the many forms of support for beginning teachers that they need to grow into proficient professionals. Only the most durable survive the first few years, especially in our cities and the rate of growth toward proficiency is far slower than it could be, at great cost to our children (see Chapter One).

PREFACE

In these pages, we provide a map for planning a comprehensive induction program for beginning teachers in their first three years of practice. This comprehensive program includes seven components:

1. A district-wide planning process that designs and then provides for the management and assessment of the induction program

2. Criteria based selection and matching of mentors

3. Services for mentors: training, supervision, support

4. Services for beginning teachers: courses, support groups, resources, feedback, coaching

5. School board and community understanding and support that is visible through budgets and policies

6. Strategies for administrators: enlisting the whole staff to support new teachers

7. On-going and well-designed program assessment

This book describes in detail the roles that district and school leaders play in a well-designed and comprehensive induction program. It provides practical recommendations and strategies that will help them to understand the vision, anticipate the stages of the process, and prepare to adapt this model to their own district circumstances.

Such a program is within the grasp of any American district now. In addition, induction programs help to strengthen the contributions of new teachers when they participate in districts' learning communities. While some districts will need to start one component at a time, we hope all districts will embrace and benefit from the comprehensive induction program that we describe in this book.

ACKNOWLEDGEMENTS

The development of an effective, comprehensive model for the induction of beginning teachers needs to be based in real practice in large, small, urban and rural school districts. We are very appreciative of the many school administrators who have welcomed us into their districts to help facilitate the development of district induction plans and the implementation of their induction programs. The suggestions, creative thinking, and cautions of these educators have greatly enhanced our thinking about this model.

We also have appreciated the thoughtful critiques of the individuals who have generously given of their time to review this book or its first edition:

Members of the *Teachers*[21] Board of Directors:

Lynn Stuart, former principal of the Cambridgeport School in Cambridge (MA) and a member of the National Commission on Teaching and America's Future

Matt King, Superintendent of the Wellesley (MA) Public Schools and a *Teachers*[21] consultant

Lyndy Johnson, Assistant Dean of Graduate Education, Simmons College and co-founder of the Beginning Teacher Center of *Teachers*[21] and Simmons College

Other *Teachers*[21] consultants and staff:

Peg Mongiello, Principal, Blake Middle School in Medfield (MA)

Rob Traver, Principal, Massachusetts Academy for Math and Science

Jennifer Antonucci, former Assistant Principal, North Middlesex Regional High School (MA)

Paul Akoury, Director of Research, *Teachers*[21]

Our colleagues in other educational organizations:

Kathleen Kelley, Former President of the Massachusetts Federation of Teachers

Donald Rebello, Former President, Massachusetts Secondary School Administrators Association and Principal of Somerset (MA) High School

Caroline Tripp, Director of Curriculum, Research for Better Teaching

We are grateful to our office manager, **Dan Price**, who provided ongoing logistical support and technology expertise for the development of this book. Thanks, also, to **Jill Dorval Winitzer**, our creative graphic designer, whose good judgment, skillful eye, and patience contributed to the final product.

CHAPTER ONE

Why Comprehensive Induction?

Since the middle of the 1990s, educators in America have been worried about the need to have an adequate supply of new teachers to meet the demand that was anticipated. School leaders across the country watched and read about several trends:

- Large numbers of cherished, veteran teachers, who had been in schools since the 1970s, were just a few years away from retirement.

- School populations were expanding as the baby-boomers - and their offspring - were having children in record numbers.

- Teacher education programs were not graduating the hundreds of thousands of new teachers who would be needed each year.

In 1996, the National Commission on Teaching and America's Future published *What Matters Most: Teaching and America's Future*, a major report on the conditions of teaching in America. This report predicted accurately that, between 1995 and 2005, 30 - 50% of the teachers newly hired in schools would leave their positions after just three to five years of teaching. The report also anticipated that poor and minority children would be the most likely to experience a "parade" of inexperienced teachers - year after year - because up to 50% of all new teachers in their schools would leave the district or leave the profession in their first three years of teaching.

As we entered the 2000s, it became clear to researchers and observers that the conventional wisdom was somewhat askew. America did not have a teacher supply problem; rather, it had a teacher - and administrator - retention problem (Ingersoll, 2001; Darling-Hammond and Sykes, 2003; and others). The focus on attracting new teachers needed to be transformed into a focus on preventing teacher turnover. Teachers who entered the profession through schools of education that had lowered their standards, "alternative" teacher certification routes, and "emergency" or "quick fix" programs were leaving schools or the profession within the first 3-5 years of teaching (Darling-Hammond and Sykes, 2003). Too often, these under-prepared teachers started out their careers in districts that had the most disadvantaged students. Year after year, the children who most needed high quality teaching were in classrooms led by a series of minimally prepared teachers who lacked the knowledge, skills, and experience they needed to become high quality teachers.

The Supply-Demand Conundrum

Many national and local organizations rushed in to fill the gap with the development of alternative teacher preparation and licensure programs. These programs provided "fast-track" options that provided a cursory introduction to the basics of curriculum and instruction or offered workshops on teaching that were held while the newcomers were also struggling with the day-to-day realities of their classrooms.

Teachers who entered the profession without student teaching experience have left the profession at twice the rate of those who have had experience as student teachers. Programs that recruit directly from the "prestigious" colleges, assuming that content knowledge is the primary variable in good teaching, have seen attrition as high as 80% in the first three years of the recent graduate's teaching career. Without strong grounding in instructional methods, child development, and learning theory, these new teachers flounder and become disenchanted with their newly chosen profession (Darling-Hammond and Sykes, 2003; Henke et al, 2000; NCTAF, 2003).

The conundrum is that the nation is producing enough teachers annually to meet the demand. However, many schools and districts are not able to hold onto their veteran teachers or to retain their newer teachers. Schools serving poor and minority students have turnover rates as high as 50% across the country. Suburban and rural districts have turnover figures that range from 20 - 30%. Recent research is demonstrating that not all of these teachers are leaving the profession; some of them are "migrating" to other districts or schools. Whether children - especially in high-poverty areas - are in schools with a high proportion of teachers who are the "leavers" or the "movers," the impact on the children is the same. For many of their school years they are in classrooms with teachers who are new to the district and the culture of the school or new to the skills of instruction and classroom management (Darling-Hammond and Sykes, 2003; Ingersoll 2001; Henke, et all., 2000).

The Factors Behind Teacher Attrition

New and veteran teacher turnover - whether from the leavers or the movers, impacts schools in cities, suburbs, and rural areas across the country. Numerous researchers report that, at a disproportional rate, "teachers are transferring out of schools with poor, minority and low-achieving students" (Ingersoll, 2001; Lankford, Loeb & Wyckoff, 2002; Hanushek, Kain,& Rivkin, 2001; Scafidi, Sjoquist & Stinebrickner, 2002).

We should not be surprised. Public education and the profession of teaching are undergoing many changes. Teaching has become an increasingly complex, difficult, and demanding job. Local, state, and national reforms are setting higher standards for student achievement and greater accountability for classroom teachers. Today's teacher works with a broad spectrum of learners in his or her classroom. The "inclusion" programs in schools require teachers to provide meaningful learning experiences for a wide continuum of learners. At the same time, the classroom teacher feels the stress of state-wide testing programs that are linked to state-developed curriculum frameworks. Assessment and accountability are watchwords that drive daily performance – and breed fear and anger in the hearts of many teachers. New and veteran teachers seek support and collegial engagement as they meet the demands of 21st century schools.

A Comprehensive Approach to New Teacher Induction

Richard Ingersoll, who was one of the first researchers to point out the supply-demand conundrum, noted in 2001 that:

...widely publicized school staffing problems are not solely - or even primarily - the result of too few teachers being recruited and trained. Instead, the data indicate that school staffing problems are to a significant extent a result of a revolving door, where large numbers of teachers depart teaching long before retirement.

It is the need to retain both new and veteran teachers that has motivated many schools and districts to implement comprehensive induction programs. In prior decades, it was the principal who took responsibility for orienting and supporting new teachers. In today's schools, 20% of the staff may have recently retired and as many as 60% of the teachers in schools may be in their first three years of teaching. Most principals do not have the time or energy to provide the nurturing, support, and feedback that is essential to retaining both new and veteran teachers in today's challenging school environments.

Induction is commonly thought of as one-on-one mentoring of a new teacher by a veteran. However, to be effective, mentoring must be surrounded by a constellation of activities for all of the stakeholders involved. Comprehensive induction programs include training for the mentor, a variety of support programs for new teachers that complement and extend the mentor relationship, administrative support for the mentor program, and a district or school comprehensive induction plan that formalizes and quantifies the expectations for the induction program. Experienced, well-trained mentor teachers who know how to develop problem solving and reflection skills in new teachers can tip the balance toward their staying in or leaving their classrooms.

Induction and the Professional Learning Community

Because today's schools are characterized by high teacher turnover, a profoundly increasing knowledge base, a diverse student body, and accelerated demands for accountability, there is a strong need to build a sense of professional community. To meet the challenges of the modern classroom, teachers must become members of learning communities that share their expertise with each other, jointly take responsibility for student learning, and continuously build and expand their knowledge base. By connecting with a network of teachers who are working together to strengthen teaching and learning in their classrooms, new and veteran teachers will expand their knowledge base and build isolation-breaking personal and professional bonds that make teaching the rewarding and valuable career they expected it to be.

Comprehensive induction programs should be aimed at integrating new teachers into the community of adult learners in the building and the school district. The mentor-protégé pairing provides an important first step. The experienced mentor teacher provides an emotional and professional "safety-net" that orients and supports the new teacher with lesson planning, classroom management, parent communication, collegial relations, and the day-to-day managerial requirements. However, experience and research are demonstrating that the model of one-on-one mentoring is not enough; too many good teachers are still leaving the profession. Induction programs that integrate structured learning experiences, open classroom visitations, and teachers' study groups bring new and veteran teachers together to build and strengthen themselves as a community of educators.

Building Structures that Support Comprehensive Induction Programs

Effective induction programs require planning, commitment, and careful monitoring. The informal programs of decades past worked because a school welcomed one or two new teachers every three or four years. They relied on the initiative, instincts, and good will of teachers who may have been in the building for decades. In today's schools, few of the long-timers remain and high percentages of teachers are still developing their own expertise.

More than in years past, induction programs need to formalize the relationships among mentors and protégés so that there are clear guidelines and expectations for the relationships. Mentors ask what the district expects of them as transmitters of the culture and wisdom of teaching. Experience shows that most mentors need training and support in the critical role that they play in helping new teachers use their energy, enthusiasm, idealism, and intelligence in ways that promote student learning. Mentors and protégés want to be supported with school-based structures that promote active reflection and inquiry into teaching. They seek multiple opportunities for sharing with and learning from each other and their colleagues.

Beginning teachers are looking for indications that the district values their efforts to become quality teachers. They want assurances that they are not being left on their own to discover the mysteries of teaching. They ask if there is a system in place - and a plan - that has been designed to support and respect them as professionals and as newcomers who have more to learn.

Administrators have many unique opportunities to protect and support the mentor-protégé pair. Through scheduling, student placement, the locations of classrooms, and the assignment of duties and extracurricular activities, principals and department heads are able to impact the nature of the mentoring relationship. Administrators also can signal to their staff, through their use of resources, the importance they place on supporting the professional growth of all teachers in the building. Drawing on their own leadership skills, and on the leadership of teachers, they can nurture the development of a professional learning community that enhances and retains its teachers.

CHAPTER TWO

A Model for the Comprehensive Induction of Beginning Teachers in Their First Three Years of Teaching

Teachers[21] has developed a **comprehensive model for the induction of beginning teachers** that has been used effectively by numerous school districts. It suggests that systematic support for new teachers become a priority for school administrators. The model is based on the development of a plan that coherently brings together the many ways that schools must support their newest staff members so that they will be effective classroom teachers. It describes ways that others in the school community – veteran mentor teachers, administrators, other staff at the school – must understand their responsibility for reaching out to new teachers, including them in the school's learning community, and providing them with the encouragement, resources, beliefs, and attitudes that will contribute to their success in the classroom.

A Comprehensive Approach

It was clear to Superintendent Clare Ramirez and Assistant Superintendent Deborah Wong in 2002 that the Glendale Public Schools were going to be hiring record numbers of new teachers in the next five years. It was also clear that they would be competing with their neighboring communities for the candidates they wanted for their classrooms. To respond to this need and to ensure that the candidates they hired were successful in their schools, they formed a steering committee to develop a comprehensive induction plan for the district that would attract and retain new teachers and build a foundation for the development of a professional learning community in the school. The superintendent, others from central office, school principals, the president of the teachers association, and veteran teachers participated in a workshop on the research on mentoring programs. This training included an orientation to the needs and stages of beginning teachers, the responsibilities and skills of mentors, and activities that would engage new and veteran teachers as colleagues in learning.

With this knowledge as a foundation, the group participated in a planning process that identified goals for the district induction program, criteria for matching beginning teachers with veterans, standards and responsibilities for mentors, expectations for the mentor-protégé pair, and training and other forms of professional support for the new teachers and their mentors. With this plan in place, the Glendale schools are providing new teachers and their veteran colleagues with a coherent program of professional growth that is attracting strong candidates, strengthening the performance of newcomers, revitalizing veteran staff, and enhancing student achievement.

The Philosophical Underpinnings

Mentoring programs are not new. For decades, principals have asked respected veteran teachers to be mentors to newcomers. Once they were paired, the mentor and the protégé were basically left on their own to carve out a relationship that was satisfying and useful. Rarely were they formally linked to other resources in the school and rarely did other folks in the school feel that they had a responsibility to the new teachers - since they "already had a mentor."

When they participated in informal mentoring programs, new teachers reported that they felt they were a burden to their mentors. How often might the mentor want to hear the problems and complaints of the new teacher? How much of their mentor's time could the new teacher expect to take? At the same time, mentors were not sure of the role they should play with the new teachers. They had been told that they were in a confidential relationship, but they wondered how well this relationship was understood by the principal and others in the school. They were sometimes reluctant to provide ideas or suggestions because they did not want to be perceived "as supervisors."

The current, enlightened approach to mentoring recognizes that new teachers are rarely prepared for the demanding job of teaching in contemporary schools. New teachers who are supported by a mentor and a network of supportive colleagues are more likely to remain in their schools and in the profession long enough to "hit their stride" as teachers. It is a tragic waste of resources when good people come into teaching with great intentions and then are left to "figure it out" on their own. These potential educators are lost to the profession and, more importantly, the children in their classrooms lose out. Numerous research reports indicate that children who are taught by under-prepared and unsupported teachers year after year do less well than children who have teachers with strong backgrounds in content areas *and* teaching approaches. Similarly, research continues to demonstrate that teacher quality is the essential ingredient in student achievement (Hanushek et al, 2005).

What is Meant by a "Comprehensive" Approach?

The *Teachers*[21] comprehensive induction model presents an enhanced vision for induction:

| The success of the beginning teacher is the responsibility of all staff in the building. | And the corollary statement | No one mentor should have the responsibility of meeting all of the needs of his/her protégé. |

The model assumes that the school wants to become a professional learning community in which all staff know that they play an essential role in the success of the beginning teacher - and of each other. With this understanding in place, we can expect to see...

- *Teachers welcoming new and veteran teachers into their classrooms as they "make teaching public."*

- *Teachers sharing curriculum materials and learning tools from their file drawers so that beginning teachers do not need to spend the first few years "reinventing the wheel."*

- *Teams of teachers conferring with each other on strategies for meeting the needs of specific students.*

- *Teams of teachers sharing their approaches to classroom management and discipline.*

- *School administrators working with teachers to develop organizational structures, find time, and nurture leadership so that the school becomes a professional learning community.*

To achieve this vision, it is essential to engage a broad base of school administrators and teachers in developing a plan for a comprehensive induction program. This induction program cannot depend on the initial enthusiasm of a few dedicated administrators or teachers for its survival. It can only become institutionalized when it is an integral part of the professional development program and budget of the district.

The heart of a comprehensive model of induction is the plan, as can be seen in Figure 1. Through the process of planning, a comprehensive program is designed that provides support and guidelines for all of the key stakeholders in the new teacher's success.

- Representatives from all of the constituencies in the school engage in a **broadly-based planning process** that delineates criteria, qualifications, and standards for the induction program. This plan should be flexible, so that it can respond to changing conditions with input from the appropriate constituencies. (See sample plan in Appendix A.)

- A coherent program of **staff development and collegial networking** is designed for mentors, beginning teachers, other school and district staff, and school and district administrators. This training and networking for teachers and administrators deepens their **knowledge base on teaching and builds a professional learning community for beginning and veteran teachers.**

- **Mentors** participate in workshops that strengthen their skills in providing positive and negative feedback to colleagues. They also update and refine their knowledge base on the district curriculum and on the latest research on teaching and learning.

- **Beginning teachers** attend workshops on classroom management, curriculum, and teaching strategies that bridge the gaps that so often emerge between their teacher preparation programs and the realities of the first three years of teaching.

- A **professional community of learners** develops or is enhanced as mentor-pairs share ideas on curriculum and instruction, engage in reflections on teaching, and participate in formal and informal observations in each others' and other colleagues' classrooms. These collegial interactions support the new teachers and strengthen the culture of the school as a learning community.

- **Superintendents, principals, and other school administrators** participate in institutes that focus on the unique opportunities they have to build a school culture in which all of the staff take shared responsibility for student and adult learning in the school and the district. They expand their understanding of strategies for facilitating colleague-to-colleague observing, conferencing, reflecting, and planning. They receive training on techniques for ensuring that the excellent candidates they hired receive developmentally appropriate supervision and evaluation.

- **School board members** receive information that briefs them on the significance and design of comprehensive induction and professional learning communities. They are asked to form policies and budgets to support the program.

- **Communications** are essential to a strong induction program. Using newsletters, cable-tv, web pages, letters home, and articles in the local newspaper that broadcast the benefits of their induction program, district and school leaders get the message out to the schools and the community. Teachers, administrators, parents, students, and others in the community learn about the goals and objectives of the induction program and understand why it is a valuable asset of the school district.

- **Formal and informal ongoing evaluation** ensures that the program is meeting the needs of beginning teachers and mentors, strengthening teaching and learning in schools, and retaining both new and veteran teachers.

TEACHERS[21]
Model for the Comprehensive Induction of Beginning Teachers

Criteria Based
Selection and Matching
of Mentors

Mentor Services

• Training

• Supervision & Support

Beginning Teacher Services

• Beginning Teacher Courses

• Beginning Teacher Support Groups

**District Wide
Planning Process**

• Central Office

• Administrators

• Teachers Union

• New & Veteran Teachers

Administrator Services

• Strategies for
Whole Faculty Involvement

• Skills for the
Supervision & Development
of Beginning Teachers

• Support for Mentors

**School Board &
Community Development**

Education, Policy
and Financial Support

**On-going Program
Assessment**

Foundations for the Model:
• Professional Knowledge Base on Teaching
• Constant Strengthening of the Professional Learning Community

Figure 1.

CHAPTER THREE

The Components of a Comprehensive Induction Program

The Teachers[21] model for the comprehensive induction of new teachers has seven components. This chapter provides information, ideas, and strategies that enable a district to select an approach for initiating or revitalizing an induction program and take advantage of its current experience base with mentoring.

- *Perhaps new teachers are paired with mentors, but no training is provided.*

- *Perhaps mentors are being provided with a stipend for training, but have no guidelines on how often they should be meeting with their new teacher - and what these meetings should entail.*

- *Perhaps the district once had a program - but its commitment has dwindled.*

Revisiting and Revitalizing the District Induction Plan

Newly hired assistant superintendent, Alicia Hernandez, was asked by her superintendent to oversee - and perhaps revitalize - the district's mentor program. Alicia searched the files and found a "Plan for the Induction of New Teachers" that was developed over 5 years ago. She asked some principals and teachers, a few of whom were hired in the past 5 years, what they knew about the program. Her research revealed that a few principals and veteran teachers remembered that the district once had a strong program. Although the district was no longer offering training for mentors, a few principals had continued to ask veteran teachers to mentor newcomers.

Alicia asked a few principals who were supportive of the induction program, some veteran teachers who had served as mentors, and some new teachers to join her in rebuilding the district induction program. This team reviewed the plan and engaged in some research on the elements in effective induction programs. They recommended changes that reflected the realities of the district in 2006 and provided suggestions for renewing the program in the next school year.

Component 1:
District-Wide Planning Process

At the heart of a comprehensive induction program is the plan. Whether a district is launching a new program or strengthening a program that may have languished, the first step is to assemble stakeholders who will set goals, design activities, and identify tasks and timelines for the program.

The Stakeholders

The district plan for the induction of new teachers belongs to many people. These stakeholders must be represented in the process of conceptualizing and developing the plan.

Who are these stakeholders and why should they be involved?

Superintendents, school boards, and central office staff

Superintendents and other district administrators - and the school board - are key players in demonstrating the district's commitment to the plan. Their understanding of and support for the program are essential in ensuring that needed resources flow in its direction.

Many districts establish the position of **Program Coordinator** to oversee the operations of the program. This position may be full time in a large district or the responsibility of a lead teacher or administrator in a smaller district.

continued...

continued from previous page...

Teachers Association

Teachers associations want to be partners with superintendents and others in the administration to ensure that their new members receive the support and encouragement they will need to be effective and successful in the classroom. Professionalizing teaching means joint ownership and accountability for the quality of teaching by unions and administrators. The teachers association should be represented on the comprehensive induction planning and steering committees.

Veteran Teachers

Because mentoring is a key component of most induction programs, it is important that veteran teachers play a role in shaping the decisions that will impact them and their colleagues.

Beginning Teachers

Teachers with one or two years of experience in the school or district are a valuable source of information on the needs and daily realities of brand new teachers.

Principals

Principals are perhaps the key constituency in determining the success and effectiveness of new teachers and of an induction program.

Principal input - from every building in the district - into the macro and micro issues that are addressed by the plan is essential if the district is to develop a plan that will have the support of building leaders. The actions and attitudes of the school principal are key in modeling the kind of support for beginning teachers that is expected from all staff. Principals have opportunities to "walk their talk" through their actions. These opportunities emerge from scheduling that provides new and veteran teachers with common times for planning and "opposing" times for observations; the assignment of students to the new teachers' classrooms; and the extracurricular expectations that are placed on new teachers. The decisions that principals make regarding the resources they uniquely control - such as time and scheduling - give powerful messages to other staff about what the principal values and supports.

The Planning Process

Most districts find that they can develop an initial draft of a plan in approximately two full days of intensive work. The goal of the planning committee is to develop a **framework** that outlines the district's approaches to the induction of beginning teachers. This framework should have sufficient flexibility to enable staff in individual buildings to make modifications that reflect the uniqueness of each school community. These modifications could relate to the process for the selection and matching of mentors and protégés, the frequency of mentor networking meetings, staff development activities, or other aspects of the program.

Districts that already have an informal support program for new teachers may want to start with a self-assessment of the strengths that exist in its schools. Appendix D provides a sample of a self-assessment tool that can be used to initiate the needs assessment process.

The planning process for developing a comprehensive induction plan can be described as an **inverted pyramid**. The process starts by developing global understandings about the mission and goals of the induction program and, in a series of steps, narrows down its focus to the very concrete specifics of the district plan.

While there is great variation in the comprehensive induction plans that districts develop, they usually contain the following elements:

1. **A mission or vision statement**

   The process of developing a **succinct** vision statement helps to confirm the group's mutual understanding of the program. It also provides a statement that can be used to describe the program on recruitment brochures, in teachers' handbooks, on the district website.

Samples:

> The purpose of the beginning teacher induction program is to provide professional and emotional support for the beginning teacher through mentoring and other parallel structures. The results of our program will be the rapid growth of expertise among beginning teachers, increased collegiality among staff, and enhanced student learning.

> The purpose of the XYZ Public Schools induction program for new teachers is to create a cadre of professionals who will enhance the quality of education for children. The program will result in building a positive, supportive, and interactive learning environment for all educators and learners.

Although the process of developing a mission or vision is critically important, planners should use a time-efficient approach. Most of the planning time should be spent on the details of the plan itself.

2. Goals for the induction program

It is likely that the language used in induction plans will place a heavy focus on the factors that enhance new teachers' success and enrich the quality of new teachers' experience in schools. While the existence of a congenial and collegial environment is important to the recruitment and retention of teachers, it is not the whole picture.

Induction programs are first and foremost about improving student performance by strengthening teaching and learning in the classroom. School districts are encouraged to develop goal statements that reflect the balance between outcomes for students (enhanced learning) and outcomes for new *and* veteran teachers (a school culture that supports collegial professional growth).

3. A communications plan

Many comprehensive induction programs are among the "best kept secrets" of the district. A communications plan helps the district to promote the program as a **valuable asset** that helps to attract and retain excellent teachers. It is a resource for administrators and others whose responsibilities include teacher recruitment, community awareness, and district public relations.

A communications plan outlines:

- WHAT folks in the community need to know about the district's induction program

- WHO in the community should know about the program

- HOW existing communication vehicles can be used to inform the community about the program

4. Roles and responsibilities

The plan delineates the roles and responsibilities of the major players in a comprehensive induction program. These roles and responsibilities may vary from district to district. The descriptions are helpful in describing the expectations that are held for teachers, administrators, union leaders, school committees, parents, and all others who have a stake in the success of beginning teachers.

In defining the roles and responsibilities, districts can differentiate the areas of responsibility that rest with central office administrators - the superintendent and the mentor coordinator - and the decisions that are made at the building level by principals and school staff.

- In some districts, all training for mentors and beginning teachers is coordinated at the central office; in others, staff development programs are organized at the building level.

- New teacher orientation programs may be coordinated at the district or building levels, or a combination of both.

- The process for selecting and matching mentors varies across districts and, sometimes, across buildings in a district.

- The superintendent, the school committee, and the teachers association play a vital role in setting the tone for the program. While the expectations may differ from plan to plan, these leaders should be visible in promoting, advancing, and advocating for the program in their districts.

5. **Training and networking**

A comprehensive induction program includes training for mentors and new teachers. It also provides workshops for administrators that provide strategies and suggestions for supporting new teachers. The induction plan provides a multi-year outline of the goals, content, and timeframes for this professional development.

6. **Selection, matching, and other specific aspects of the mentoring program**

The "nuts and bolts" of the mentor-pairing program are a key component of any plan. This section of the plan outlines the process for selecting and matching mentors and protégés, the frequency of conferences and classroom visitations, the district policy on confidentiality, the ways that mentors are recognized and rewarded, and other operational aspects of the mentor-pairing program.

7. **Recognition and appreciation of mentors**

The plan should explicitly describe the ways that mentors will be provided with recognition and compensation for the important work they are doing. Most school districts provide stipends for mentors as well as other forms of recognition and appreciation.

8. **Piloting the program**

The size of the district sometimes determines whether a comprehensive induction program is launched initially in every school or as a pilot in a few schools. It may determine whether all components of the plan are implemented at the same time or are phased in over time.

9. **Program assessment**

A commitment to engage in ongoing assessment of the effectiveness of the induction plan is essential to improvement and success. Plans should outline the information that will be gathered - and by whom - and the uses that will be made of this information. Mentors, protégés, and others can provide valuable insights that can strengthen even the best program.

Approval and Adoption of the Comprehensive Induction Plan

In most districts, the group that develops the plan, sometimes called the Steering Committee, sends a final draft of the plan to the superintendent's office and the union leadership. Once there is agreement on all of the points in the plan, it is sent to the school board. Local practice may differ on whether the school board reviews, accepts, or adopts the plan. The goal is to have school board members understand the plan, support its goals and approaches, recognize the financial and other resource implications of the plan, and serve as its "cheerleaders."

Component 2:
Criteria Based Selection and Matching of Mentors

Signal High Standards

Not every teacher has the temperament, skills, or time to be a mentor. We recommend that teachers be required to apply for the position of mentor and that the selection process be linked to high standards. This process starts with circulating criteria and expectations that describe this important responsibility. It signals to potential mentors - and other staff - the importance of this role and the high regard in which it is held at the school and district levels.

Mentoring programs are most successful when they are inclusive and provide all teachers with the opportunity to participate. Veteran teachers should be invited to attend an orientation meeting that describes the roles and expectations for mentors. Current mentors, or teachers who have informally mentored in the past, may be invited to talk about what it has meant to them to support a new teacher. While not all teachers who apply and who participate in the orientation may be selected in a given year to become mentors, the process helps them understand the expectations of mentors and the ways that they can support new teachers in their schools. At the same time, superintendents, principals, and other administrators should feel free to urge individuals whom they believe have the appropriate knowledge, skills, and attitudes to apply to become a mentor.

Districts may want to consider the following sample criteria and expectations for mentors.

Criteria

- Proven track-record as a successful classroom teacher with over three years experience

- A communication style that adapts to individual differences

- Evidence of a commitment to constant learning about the skills and craft of teaching

- A commitment to collegiality with peers and to experimentation in one's teaching

- Demonstrated perseverance and confidence building with resistant students and slow learners

- Strong belief that effective effort is the key determinant of student success

- Ability to make a long-term commitment to the protégé and to the mentoring role

- Commitment to the completion of a program of study that builds mentoring skills in observing and analyzing teaching, diagnosing problems, and communicating about the strategies of skillful teaching

Expectations

Mentors are expected to:

- Complete a 36-hour course on mentor skill training in the first year of mentoring

- Engage in advanced mentor training in subsequent years

- Be available for a total of approximately 2 to 3 hours per week to work with protégés

  Comment: We suggest that flexible measures be applied to the requirement for 2 to 3 hours of contact per week. It is not necessary to schedule three hours of meetings. It is important that mentors connect with beginning teachers frequently, especially in the first months of school, to ask "how things are going." Mentors should find time to catch up on successes, on problems, and bolster confidence when needed. In any given week, these interactions are likely to add up to two to three hours of time.

- Observe protégés or in their classrooms at least monthly.

- Schedule one-on-one conferences with protégés - approximately once a week - to check in and address any problems or issues. These conferences should be scheduled and not preclude conversations in the hall or other brief and informal (though valuable) check-ins that will inevitably take place during the day. The purpose of these meetings is to meet protégés' - not mentors' or supervisors' - agendas.

- Rotate turns with other mentors in leading monthly seminars on topics of concern or interest to the protégés as a group (e.g., parent conferences, back-to-school night, classroom discipline, or the curriculum of a specific content area). Seminars can be scheduled on "early release days," staff development in-service days, or for study group sessions.

- Demonstrate lessons or management techniques on request.

- Link beginning teachers with other resource people in the school and district.

- Maintain relationships with beginning teachers through their second and third years of teaching if the district has a three-year provision in its plan.

Maintain Logs

An additional expectation for mentors and protégés is that they maintain time logs of their meetings, classroom visitations, and other professional interactions to demonstrate that they have met the "time" standard that is set by the district. These logs can be maintained in teachers' date books and later transcribed into a report for the district. Some districts also ask for a one or two word description of the focus of the meetings or classroom visitations (e.g., curriculum development, classroom management, parent communication). This information provides the district with data on potential problem areas for all new teachers while not breaching the confidentiality of the mentoring relationship. If district leaders see that "parent conferencing" appears frequently on mentor-protégé logs, they may decide that they should schedule training for new teachers on parent communication.

Sample Mentoring Log

Date	Time	Topic
8/28	9:15 - 9:45	Start up issues
8/29	2:30 - 3:00	Parent involvement
9/7	7:45 - 8:00 3:15 - 3:30	Classroom management
9/9	8:05 - 8:30	Rules and routines
10/4	2:30 - 3:00	Back to school night
10/6	7:30 - 8:00	Back to school night

Provide Time and Recognition for Mentors

Veteran teachers who are considering applying to be a mentor will want to know how they will be supported in this role. As a part of the orientation for new mentors, districts will want to be prepared to address this reasonable concern.

There are a number of ways that districts can support mentors.

• *Provide compensatory or relief time*
Mentors' planning, preparing, and teaching loads are usually not reduced when they become mentors. Districts can relieve mentors

of duties (e.g., bus duty, recess supervision, study halls, detention) to provide the time that the job of mentoring demands.

• *Offer stipends and other recognition*
Stipends should represent a meaningful amount of compensation because mentors represent the highest level of professional excellence in the district. In addition, they are supporting a most important asset of the school district, its newest staff members. We recommend that stipends are set at approximately 5% of a teacher's base pay or a fixed amount that acknowledges the respect of the district and the time commitment of the position. Other forms of recognition are described in Appendix B.

Match Mentors and Protégés Carefully

The traditional wisdom on matching has stood the test of repeated research and practical experience:

When matches are based on this triad, **grade level, content area, and proximity in the building**, they provide valuable support for new teachers. Grade level and content area matches provide obvious commonality in terms of child development, classroom management, and curriculum and instruction expertise. Mentors whose classrooms are in close proximity to their protégés are able to be informally available before and after school, during hall duty, and at other "down" times during the school day. Common backgrounds, professional interests, and social and vocational interests also contribute to successful matches.

In many districts, it is the principals - who hired the new teachers and are strongly committed to their success - who make the matches with mentors. Because principals have good knowledge of the teachers in the building and of the new teachers, they often seek the responsibility for making these matches. In other districts, matching is done by a committee that includes the principal. Occasionally, an assistant superintendent or the district's mentor coordinator makes the matches in consultation with building principals.

Avoid the "Blind Date"

For too many teachers, the mentor pairing process results in a "blind date." The teachers do not know each other and neither partner has input into the pairing.

Recommendations for circumventing the blind date

- The interview team. Principals invite potential mentors for the third grade teacher or the new science teacher to participate in the interview process as members of an interview team. Through the discussion that takes place during the interview, some pairings are able to be made based on natural "affinity."

- The "sock hop" approach. New teachers and prospective mentors spend time together in workshops and social activities, often held in August, that enable them to become at least slightly acquainted. New and veteran teachers are encouraged during this time to "find comfortable partners" in their grade level or content area with whom they would like to be matched. This "pairing off" allows teachers to find colleagues with whom they have some initial "chemistry."

The "No-Fault Bail Out" Provision

What if, with the best of intentions on all sides, the match does not work? Sometimes two good teachers may find that their styles or their personalities are not a good match. The pairing is mutually unsatisfying and unsatisfactory. The "no-fault bail out" process enables the pair to talk with a neutral person - usually *not* the school principal who is their supervisor - to ask that they be reassigned to other teachers. In many districts, an assistant superintendent, a guidance counselor, or the mentor coordinator serves as this "neutral person" and may attempt to provide some mediation to the pair to determine if the match can be salvaged. If not, a new pairing is made "with no prejudice" toward the pair.

Maintain Confidentiality

A sensitive and important issue for both beginning teachers and mentors is the issue of confidentiality. Mentors should not be put in the role of evaluator or be expected to report to principals on any aspect of the performance of the beginning teacher. New teachers need to be confident they can reveal their fears, disappointments, and vulnerabilities to a trusted mentor who will use this trust as a springboard to help, not injure. Yet, there must be boundaries to confidentiality when the interest of children is at stake. Therefore, we recommend the statement below as a document that defines confidentiality between mentors and beginning teachers:

Confidentiality Statement

In general, mentors will not discuss their protégé's teaching performance with anyone, including school and district administrators, except under the following conditions:

1. Mentor teachers will be able to discuss, **with the protégé's knowledge and permission**, any aspect of their protégé's performance with other members of the mentoring team – i.e., the principal or teachers or administrators who may be designated as resources for the new teacher.

2. Mentors, **with the protégé's knowledge and permission**, may discuss the protégé's teaching performance with resource professionals whose job it is to help teachers. *(For example, if the novice needs help in designing hands on science lessons, the district science coordinator may be consulted for help and advice.)*

3. Mentors, **with the protégé's knowledge**, may discuss the protégé's teaching performance with appropriate administrators if, in the mentor's professional judgment, the academic growth and development, social well-being, or physical safety of the students is at risk.

Teachers[21]

Districts are highly encouraged to provide training to superintendents, principals, and other district administrators on the principles that underlie confidentiality so that these leaders have the same understandings as do new and veteran teachers about how the confidentiality policy works. Supervisors and evaluators should be reminded that the presence of a mentor in no way changes their responsibility to provide support and guidance to new teachers on a regular basis. They must understand that the mentor should not be expected to be a source of information on the performance of the beginning teacher. Their evaluations of new teachers must be based on their own first-hand knowledge of the new teachers' performance.

Component 3:
Services for Mentors

Before the mentor training, I was not sure I was cut out to be a mentor. How did I know that I would have the patience and skills to help a new teacher? The training helped me understand my role as a mentor and gave me opportunities to practice the kinds of conversations I was likely to have with a new teacher.

To my delight, working with Josh this year has been one of the most enlightening experiences of my career. I found that I learned as I reflected with him on my approaches to teaching - and I expanded my repertoire of strategies as he shared his ideas with me.

Mentor Teacher

There is abundant research that points to the necessity of training for mentors. While most mentors are strong classroom practitioners, this excellence does not always translate into effective mentoring. The core of support for mentors includes training on the roles and responsibilities of mentoring and on approaches to supporting beginning teachers on curriculum development, instructional strategies, positive classroom management, reflective practice, and problem solving. Mentors also benefit from workshops with other mentors in which they problem-solve and analyze case studies to expand their repertoire of skills for building rapport and collegial relationships with the protégés.

Mentor training has a double benefit in that it expands mentors' skills and knowledge base for inducting new teachers and it reinforces in these exemplary veterans the skills, knowledge, and attitudes that are essential in building a professional learning community in the school or district. In schools that are operating as learning communities, mentors can take the opportunity of mentoring to transmit the culture to the new teachers. In schools that are aspiring to become learning communities, mentors can become teacher leaders who help the school and the district to create a culture of collegial sharing and learning.

Training: Nine Modules

Figure 2 presents nine topical areas that we recommend as essential blocks for mentor training. While the sequence is not critical, it does have a rationale and seeks to ensure that the mentor has the knowledge base, skills, and attitudes needed to support and retain the next generation of teachers. It is useful for mentors to have completed at least Module 1, which requires 9 hours, before they take on the responsibility of working with a beginning teacher. In the first year of mentoring, mentors will want to participate in the remaining 27 hours of training that address topics in Modules 2 - 9. In the second and subsequent years, mentors can expand their skills through 36 hours of training in more advanced topics that are outlined in Figure 2.

The **first module** provides important baseline information about the roles and responsibilities of the mentor. It examines research on the needs and developmental stages of individuals who are new to teaching and the impact that good mentoring relationships have on the success and retention of beginning teachers. Prospective mentors review the principles surrounding confidentiality and learn about the linkages among mentoring, collegiality, and professional learning communities.

The **second module** explores communication styles that mentors will find useful when problem solving with protégés, veteran colleagues, and other people in their lives, such as family members and friends. Mentors find it informative and interesting to explore the diverse thinking and communication styles that different people use to identify and solve problems. For example:

- *Some people like to generate masses of alternative solutions before beginning to weigh what should be done.*

- *Others want to linger over the definition of a problem and a vision of the outcomes that could result from the solution before spending time in brainstorming ideas.*

- *Some people think through their ideas by talking out loud without intending to signify that they have taken a position; they may sound like they're taking a position, but they're only thinking aloud.*

- *Other people do their thinking and sorting inside their head, and only speak when they do have a position which they want to float.*

These examples are just a sampling of a larger constellation of variables that come into play for people during problem solving. Two teachers with opposite styles can find that they are not productive in problem solving together - or can get into unnecessary conflicts if they don't understand their partner's communication style. There are a number of frameworks upon which communication training can be based. We recommend Harrison and Bramson's model (Harrison and Bramson, 1982) because it focuses on communication between people working on problems in the work setting.

Mentor Skill Training
72 hours over 2 years of Basic and Advanced Training

Module 1– Roles of Mentors

The needs and stages of beginning teachers

The mentor-protégé relationship (e.g., confidentiality, collegiality)

Rapport and trust

Overview of mentoring skills

Belief systems for high performing teachers

Comprehensive induction programs

Professional learning communities

9 hours

Module 2 – Communication Styles

Thinking styles, problem solving styles

Matching communication styles to the protégé

6 hours

Module 3 – Differential Conferencing

(includes basic and advanced topics)

Developing the relationship through support, help, and problem solving

Differential leadership styles

Modeling and role-playing 3 kinds of conferences: non-directive, collaborative, directive

Case studies on matching conferencing styles along the collaborative/directive continuum

Using data to define the problem

Active listening & probing for specificity in problem solving conferences

Role-plays of problem solving

Feedback exercise from cognitive coaching

Focus on directive conferencing and delivering negative information

18 hours

Module 4 – Developing Protégé's Planning Skills

Alignment of objectives, learning experiences, and assessment

Alignment with curriculum frameworks

Backwards planning:

Using this approach to planning

Coaching and helping others to use it

12 hours

Module 5 – Diagnosing and Solving Planning & Management Problems

Space, time, routine momentum, attention, expectations and consequences, motivation

9 hours

Module 6 – Advocacy

Helping protégés deal with:

1. principals 2. difficult people
3. conflicts with other staff 4. their role in the school

3 hours (advanced)

Module 7 – Planning

Action plan by month

6 hours (advanced)

Module 8 – Guardian of Values

Responsibility and accountability

Personal efficacy

Constant learning

Mission, repertoire and matching

Collegiality and interdependence

6 hours (advanced)

Module 9 – The Professional Learning Community

Working with administrators and mentor leaders

Induction and the professional learning community

3 hours (advanced)

Figure 2.

The **third module** devotes a significant amount of time to "differential conferencing." Once mentors have developed a good sense of the communication styles of their protégés, they are ready to determine the degree of directness they should be using with the beginning teacher. "Differential conferencing" refers to a continuum that describes a variety of ways that a mentor can provide feedback to a new teacher or colleague. This continuum encompasses non-directive, consultative feedback on one end, collaborative approaches in the center, and highly directive feedback at the opposite end. The style that a mentor uses is based on the mentor's assessment of the *professional* maturity of the beginning teacher. *Professional* maturity refers to a new teacher's level of experience and wisdom in decision-making within a particular field and has nothing to do with personal or emotional maturity.

Differential conferencing has a long history in the literature of supervision (e.g., Hersey, Blanchard, and Johnson, 2000; Glickman, 2000). Mentor training helps mentors develop a continuum of communication skills and gain sensitivity in *using* and knowing *when to use* these different modes. Glickman (2000) diagrams the continuum as follows:

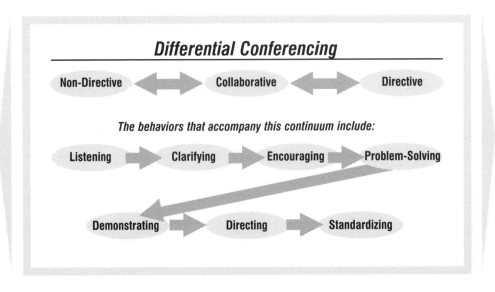

The goal of the mentor is to provide feedback and coaching that develops novices' capacity to analyze and make decisions. It is appropriate for mentors use data from classroom visitations to focus the protégés' attention on events they may have missed. It is never out of place to ask good questions to stimulate new teachers' thinking and decision making capacity. It is also appropriate, when conditions warrant, to tell protégés what to do, how to do it, and what not to do, especially if they are floundering. These decisions, when made by mentors, fall within the realm of "differential conferencing."

The **fourth module** of mentor training targets beginning teachers' planning skills. College courses and student teaching too often fall short of the mark in this area. We find that many beginning teachers have gaps in the logic and precision they bring to aligning the instructional experiences they offer and the learning objectives they have for students. Too often, the activities they design for students are not targeted toward the knowledge and skills they want students to attain.

Successful teaching is built on teachers' ability to help students understand that the activities they are asked to do can logically be expected to lead to specific student learning. The teacher's role is to communicate this image to students, ideally with exemplars of what good work will look like. In this era of high standards and accountability, we still find that too often teachers - even experienced teachers - design projects and activities for students that are engaging, real-world oriented, and fun... but not connected to the expressed learning objectives for the unit or curriculum framework. They are the teacher's favorites, or the kids' favorites, or suggestions from a teachers' guide or the web. When mentors have strong skills in lesson planning, they are able to coach new teachers on effective planning and thinking skills.

The **fifth module** addresses the vital skills of diagnosing and solving classroom management problems with beginning teachers. Just because a mentor is a good classroom manager is no guarantee that he or she can help a new teacher become proficient. Great players do not always make good coaches. This module gives mentors the skills to analyze and articulate issues related to classroom management problems. It gives them vocabulary and conceptual frameworks for helping beginning teachers understand the nature of a problem and generate new responses.

The **sixth module** prepares mentors to advocate for protégés, if necessary, and to support beginning teachers to advocate for themselves. The need for advocacy most often emerges in the context of conflicts that arise with other adults in the school community. Mentors are most comfortable in this role if they are prepared to identify the situations that may arise and to draw on the skills of honest, open communication and mediation.

The **seventh module** provides mentors with suggestions and strategies for developing a plan for their work with beginning teachers over the course of the year. Knowing the school calendar, the protégé's personal goals, and the school's priorities, mentors develop a monthly plan that parallels the needs of beginning teachers. The design of this monthly plan ensures that interactions with the beginning teacher include a balance among all of the essential issues such as classroom management, lesson planning and instruction, collegial relationships, and professionalism.

The **eighth module** has a "values-driven" dimension, even though its fruits show up concretely in very specific and practical circumstances. This module engages mentors in discussions aimed at influencing the belief systems and values of beginning teachers. This is a crucial topic because, ultimately, all teachers' decisions and actions spring from their beliefs about themselves, children's learning, what it means to be a professional, and what it means to be a member of a professional learning community. We subscribe to the following beliefs and recommend that mentors discuss them with their protégés.

Beliefs for Influencing the Next Generation of Teachers

Responsibility and Accountability

If the children aren't learning, I can't blame them or their life circumstances. It is my responsibility to keep examining my curriculum and my teaching to reach these children.

Personal Efficacy

I can be successful as a teacher and help these children experience success. I can do it.

Constant Learning

Teaching is intellectually complex, difficult, and demanding work. It is expected that I ask for help and consult colleagues frequently, both as a beginner and as a veteran. No one knows everything there is to know about teaching, or ever will. Constant learning is the name of the game.

Mission, Repertoire, and Matching

There is not one right or best way to do something in teaching. Skillful teaching means continually enlarging one's repertoire and getting ever more accurate at picking from one's repertoire to match the student, the situation, or the curriculum.

Collegiality and Interdependence

Effective professional practice requires true collegial behavior among teachers. It is expected of me and I expect it of my colleagues in return. I know that we need each other to produce effective work for children. I also know that we as a grade/department/school faculty have cumulative school-wide effects.

The **ninth module** focuses on the linkages between the induction program and the school and district as a professional learning community. Mentors expand their understanding of a comprehensive induction program and the roles of the mentor coordinator, school administrators, central office administrators, the teachers association, and other teachers in the system. They also examine models for developing professional learning communities and explore ways to ensure that the induction program is appreciated as the first step that new teachers take as they become involved with the district's community of learners.

Component 4:
Services for Beginning Teachers

As one of my questions during my interview, I asked the principal if there was a mentoring program for new teachers. She told me that she felt very strongly about the importance of pairing each new teacher with a highly respected veteran. She also told me about workshops that were designed specially for new teachers. It became clear to me that all new teachers were expected to participate in these programs for new teachers. I was delighted, because it said to me that I was not expected already to know everything I needed to know to be a good teacher.

Beginning Teacher

The Hiring Process

The induction of beginning teachers starts with the interview. As with hiring for any position, beliefs, expectations, and attitudes are first communicated in the interview.

In January 2000, *Education Week* reported that 28 states required that school districts provide an induction program for new teachers. While that number had slipped by 2005 because of funding crises in states, school districts are still committed to providing support for new teachers. In the last ten years, it has been fairly routine for teacher candidates to inquire in the interview about the existence of a support program for beginning teachers. Most teachers know about these services from their teacher preparation programs or from professional magazines and journals. Districts are eager to point to the quality of their induction programs as a "selling point" as they recruit new teachers.

Expectations for Beginning Teachers

In some districts, hiring is conditional upon the understanding that the new teacher will accept the support of a mentor and will participate in staff development programs for new teachers. In other districts, new teachers are "cordially invited" to take advantage of induction programs that have been put in place to support their successful introduction into the profession and the school district.

Mentor Pairing

During the hiring process, the district informs candidates that they will be paired with a mentor and expected to participate in programs designed to support beginning teachers. These induction activities include weekly conferences with the mentor, feedback from the mentor based on informal visits in the new teacher's classroom, periodic problem solving sessions with the mentor, and coursework designed for new teachers. Through these messages, the district conveys its strong commitment to ensuring that new teachers are successful and that they have the professional support they deserve and need as novice teachers.

The Orientation of New Teachers

District and school leaders are encouraged to pay attention to how new teachers are welcomed…

> …*into the school district*
> …*into the schools*
> …*into the fourth grade cluster or the social studies department*

New teacher orientation often complements the "welcome back session" for all staff that occurs at the start of the year. This orientation for the new staff, which extends throughout the school year, can take several forms.

- *"Just in time" training*

  Too often, new teachers start the year at district-wide meetings where they are subjected to a massive "information dump" from the administration. The meeting usually starts or ends with the distribution of large three ring binders and assorted colorful handout sheets. New teachers report that often the information has minimal relevance for them at that time - or that they can not absorb the information because of the pressure they are feeling about the start of the school year.

  School leaders are taking a cue from "just in time" training and providing information to new teachers on a schedule that matches their need for the information. Beginning of the year bulletins provide information on the start of school. At the end of September, teachers get information and guidelines for back to school nights and parent conferences. Spring testing deadlines are sent to teachers several months later, when they are ready to plan for the Spring schedule.

Recommendations

- Develop a school schedule and calendar that highlights the important dates for which teachers need to be prepared.

- Inform teachers that the requisite forms and details will be distributed closer to the time that they will be needed. See Appendix C for a sample school calendar designed for beginning teachers.

- Provide information on district policies and procedures at the building level, as it is in the school that these policies and procedures are usually implemented.

Introductions to the Local Community

The number of new teachers who live in the community in which they teach usually is less than 50%. These new employees may be strangers to the city or town.

Recommendations

- Organize a bus or van tour that points out the neighborhoods, the popular hangouts for kids, local museums, parks, and other features that can be resources for the classroom. It is equally important to point out banks, drugstores, markets, and other sites that can be time-savers and conveniences for busy new teachers.

- Provide a map of the school and give tours of the facilities. New teachers appreciate being informed about the resources in the building that they may want to use during the year.

- Invite representatives of local museums and other educational resources to attend new teacher meetings to explain the ways that their organizations can support the curriculum.

Introductions to the School Community

With many schools experiencing a turnover of 50% or more in the last five years, administrators are instituting new approaches for helping new and veteran teachers get to know each other. These approaches are also helpful to students and parents.

Recommendations

- Using scanners and computers that are available in most schools, print "face books" that are similar to the booklets that colleges develop each year for their students. Both new and veteran teachers appreciate having at their desks this handy reminder of "who's who."

- Ask all faculty members to wear nametags with their department or grade on it for the first two weeks of school to help beginning teachers get to know the staff, especially in big schools.

- Have a staff social before school starts. Provide beginning teachers with "hosts" - who may be the mentor - who will introduce them to other staff. Highlight the beginning teachers during the event.

- Hang a bulletin board near the front office with pictures of the staff so that parents and other visitors can get to know the school community.

Beginning Teacher Institute

Day 1. Creating an Effective Environment for Learning

- Develop a welcoming climate
- Organize the classroom for high performance learning
- Promote beliefs for the next generation of teachers
- Hold high expectations for all students

Day 2. The Basics of the First Day, Week, and Month

- Prepare for the first days of school
- Identify and implement initial planning and teaching tasks
- Plan classroom procedures and routines
- Use effectively the principles of time management

Day 3. Positive Classroom Management

- Use tools for successful classroom management
- Diagnose classroom discipline problems
- Motivate students with effective teaching and learning strategies

Day 4. Building Partnerships with Parents

- Communicate effectively with parents
- Help parents support their children's learning
- Create meaningful homework assignments

Day 5. Lesson Planning

- Understand the key elements in lesson planning
- Develop lessons that meet the needs and styles of diverse learners
- Provide lessons for higher order learning

Day 6. Linking Curriculum and Assessment

- Explore the (district/state) curriculum frameworks
- Align teaching, learning, and assessment
- Use multiple approaches to student assessment

In any profession, there is a body of knowledge that one needs to learn and know to be fully functioning and effective. Appendix F, *The Knowledge Base on Teaching*, outlines six areas for teaching: content knowledge; content specific pedagogy; differences in learners; parent and community relations; professional community; and generic pedagogy.

While beginning teachers can benefit from study in all of these areas, there are clear priorities. Among the first order needs are the generic pedagogical approaches that enable the teacher to be successful in the classroom, including establishing expectations for the students; developing and reinforcing rules, routines, and procedures; employing effective classroom management strategies; and building positive relationships with parents.

By mid-October, new teachers are likely to want to focus on back-to-school night and the first parent conferences. Simulated sessions, including role-plays, are invaluable in helping new teachers become more confident as they prepare for these occasions. Veteran teachers can share with beginning teachers samples of student work that they put on display for parents to examine. They can also help teachers to anticipate topics that parents may raise in these meetings.

"What do parents really want to know on back-to-school night?"

Parents want to know something about who you are.

More importantly, they want to be reassured that you know who their children are and care about them.

"What do you include in your presentations to parents on back-to-school night?"

I find that detailed outlines of the curriculum may not meet all parents' needs.

They will want to know that you are organized, have a plan, and know what you are doing.

Another focus for beginning teachers is "mastery planning." An increasing number of beginning (as well as experienced) teachers are very knowledgeable in their academic discipline and may have a broad repertoire of instructional strategies. However, they do not necessarily choose or create instructional experiences that allow children to achieve "mastery learning."

Many district and building administrators offer in-service workshops for beginning teachers that focus on aligning teaching objectives, learning experiences, and student performance assessment. This approach to lesson planning, which is also called "Backward Design" (Wiggins and McTighe, 1998), helps beginning teachers clarify for themselves what students should know and be able to do at the conclusion of lessons and units. From this vision, teachers can then design experiences which can logically be expected to lead students to "mastery learning." Regrettably, we cannot take for granted that new or veteran teachers have this skill.

Beginning Teacher Network

The **Beginning Teacher Network** is used by some districts to provide a safe place for new teachers to discuss problems such as professional conflicts with administrators, difficult interactions with parents, or their own insecurity about an aspect of their teaching. A small group of 4 - 6 teachers meets for an hour, 10 times throughout the year, in a confidential session that is designed to address their needs and to raise issues related to their professional responsibilities. These sessions may be led by an experienced practitioner from outside the school district or by a trusted veteran teacher or administrator from within the system.

Topics that are explored by the Beginning Teacher Network could include:

- Negotiating professional relationships with colleagues

- Balancing the goals of the written curriculum with the "hidden" curriculum that is advocated by administrators

- Involving parents in meaningful roles in the classroom

- Creating time and resource management plans

Support Services for Second and Third Year Teachers

Teachers who are in their second and third years will profit from staff development that expands and deepens their knowledge base and skills. With a year of experience behind them, these teachers are ready to delve more deeply into issues related to curriculum, instruction, and assessment.

Professional development that is particularly appropriate for second and third year teachers includes:

- In-depth exploration of issues of literacy and numeracy at the elementary and secondary levels through workshops and study groups

- Coaching on interdisciplinary approaches to curriculum

- Training on expanding their repertoire of content-specific pedagogical approaches

- Guided examination of data and its use in strengthening student learning

- Course work on teaching in a standards-based classroom, differentiated instruction, and students' performance assessment

- Training on team building and working collegially with peers

- Guided projects on collaborative inquiry and action research
- Building skills for teacher leadership and engaging in the school's professional learning community

Component 5:
School Board and Community Development

Districts with strong comprehensive induction programs have made their commitment to supporting new teachers an integral part of the district culture. They have built induction into their budgets and strategic plans so that funding is assured in good and bad economic times and as there is turnover on school boards. Developing this commitment may not be easy.

Communication

Nothing, as we have noted, is more important to student learning and achievement than the quality of the teachers in the classroom. District leaders have a responsibility to educate school boards about the research on the linkages among teacher quality, student performance, and strong induction programs. When school board members have these understandings, they are less likely in tough economic times to make cuts that impact teacher quality.

School leaders who are committed to supporting their staff make the case for teacher support and teacher retention as powerfully as they advocate for new buildings, additional computers, and other resources. Presentations on issues related to teacher quality top their list of priorities for meetings of the school board - and when new members join the board. They use opportunities to advocate for the induction program at neighborhood coffees, PTO meetings, and meetings with local civic leaders. They understand that it is essential to build a strong constituency for teacher quality that will resound for the school board.

Policy

We recommend that, after district leaders educate school boards about the value of the induction program, they encourage a sympathetic school board member to propose for inclusion in the board's policy manual a statement that explains that comprehensive induction is a commitment of the district. Such a policy might read as follows:

> *The superintendent will annually review the effective functioning of the district's Comprehensive Induction Program and report the current status to the School Board.*

> *The school board will ensure adequate funding for the on-going training and support structures of the induction program.*

Budget

Every school budget should have a line item labeled "Induction Programs" that becomes part of the boilerplate used for budget planning each year. In this way, the budget institutionalizes the district's commitment to comprehensive induction.

Union Support

The country's two teachers' unions, the NEA and the AFT, are strong supporters of induction programs as a means for improving teacher quality. Their web sites are filled with examples of programs that are effectively supporting new teachers in their member districts. These national leaders encourage unions at the state and local levels to partner with district and school leaders to develop and implement strong induction and mentoring programs that will assure a high-quality workforce for the country. The AFT encourages states to develop "thoughtful, comprehensive statutes" that convey to districts, schools, and beginning teachers the importance of "deep and rigorous clinical experience as the final step in teacher preparation" (AFT , 2001).

Numerous teacher contracts include language that describes the district's expectations for the induction program. This language may include the amount of the stipend for mentors and expectations for the frequency of conferencing and classroom visitations by the mentor and the protégé. Districts that include this language in their contracts are encouraged to ensure that the expectations are realistic, attuned to current conditions, and revisited occasionally. Experience has indicated that while it is useful to acknowledge the role of the mentor in contracts, unions and school committees are not well served when contract language is highly prescriptive.

Component 6:
Strategies for Administrators

Administrators: A Key to Success

There is a high school principal - a strong advocate of induction programs for new teachers - who says:

> *There are lots of things I can do to support the induction program in my building. But, there are many more things I can do to sabotage the program.*

The effectiveness and success of an induction program are to some degree dependent on the support, nurturing, modeling, and enthusiasm of school and district administrators. Administrators set the standard for the level of commitment that is made to ensure that new teachers are successful and that those who support new teachers are given the time and resources that are needed.

> *Our principal met with all of the new teachers as a group - bi-weekly in the fall and monthly in the spring - to answer our questions, share information with us, and engage us in discussions about our experiences.*
>
> *Beginning Teacher*

> *Our superintendent made it clear that supporting our new teachers was a priority for her. Mentors were given time to meet with the new teachers, both for conferences and for observing. We also met with the principal three times during the year to discuss how the mentor program was going and ways that the school could be more supportive of new teachers.*
>
> *Veteran Mentor Teacher*

Superintendents, principals, and other administrators have numerous opportunities daily to demonstrate their priorities through:

• The issues and programs to which they give their attention

• The visible, personal support they provide to programs and activities

• The areas in which they proclaim their "outrage"

• The topics to which they give priority at their meetings

Administrators' actions speak in volumes that are louder than their words. Principals and other administrators who "walk the talk" by facilitating meetings and interactions among new teachers and their mentors will find that others pick up the message and act similarly.

Start with the Interview

It is not an exaggeration to say that supporting, nurturing, retaining, and acculturating the new teacher starts with the interview with the principal. In the last decade, interviews with new teachers have shifted emphasis. The candidates are as interested in how the school and the district are prepared to help them to be successful in this new job as they are with presenting their credentials.

The interview gives administrators opportunities to:

• Share their vision about the education of children

• Describe the culture of the school - the values, beliefs, and attitudes that are shared by school staff

• Describe the staff development opportunities that are provided by the school and the district

• Outline the ways that the school supports teachers who are new to the school or new to the profession

It also provides a vehicle for launching the new teacher's involvement in the district induction program. It is most appropriate to use the interview to:

• Set expectations for new staff in regard to their participation in the activities and services of the induction program, such as workshops, meetings, and the mentor pairing program.

• Provide veteran teachers with an opportunity to meet with new teachers - as part of an interview panel or post-interview socializing, for example - to help take some of the guesswork out of the matching process.

• Demonstrate the administrator's commitment to supporting the success of new teachers by giving examples of how this support is provided.

Enlist the Whole Staff

A colleague noted that we would not need mentors if the whole staff adopted each beginning teacher as its own protégé. In this scenario, all staff would be mentors to new teachers and would work in schools that were appropriately structured for professional practice. While we believe there is a need for trained mentors who create a special relationship with individual beginning teachers, it is equally important to build a professional learning community in which all staff members "adopt" the beginning teachers.

Two questions for principals and other building leaders emerge:

What would you do if you wanted every member of your staff to believe that…

1) Every teacher in the building has a stake in the beginning teachers' success?

2) Every teacher in the building has something of value to offer the beginning teachers?

Let's get more specific. It's April. What can you do between now and next year's first new teacher orientation meeting to accomplish the two challenges listed above?

Class Placement and Scheduling

By April, administrators usually know how many openings there will be at each grade level and in each department. We urge school leaders to be very deliberate about class placement decisions so that new teachers are assigned students and classes that are appropriate to their beginner status.

This means, bluntly, that you make sure that **new teachers do not get**:

• Stripped down classrooms

• Large classes

• Difficult students

• Many preparations for each day

• A heavy load of extracurricular assignments

It also means that **new teachers do get schedules that allow for**:

• Common planning time with their mentor for conferencing and other meetings

• Opportunities to be observed by their mentor and to observe their mentor and other teachers

Ask teachers who know new teachers' students to attach personal notes - one or two sentences - that tell something useful about each of these students' learning styles, interests, or special aptitudes.

Works well in small groups, especially if you give him a leadership role. Otherwise, he might try to lead them anyway by cracking jokes.

Needs encouragement to bolster her self-esteem.

Plays a mean saxophone.

This is the kind of information that does not show up in cumulative records that are passed forward with students.

Provide and Protect Time

Beginning teachers should be excused from committee assignments to the degree possible so they can concentrate on the all-important tasks of teaching and learning to teach. Similarly, mentors should have a minimal number of committee assignments and duties so they have time for their protégé. Administrators can help mentors by allotting them time, ideally three hours a week, to devote to their beginning teacher. Superintendents and principals should collaborate with mentors and protégés to be sure that scheduled events do not conflict with either beginning teacher or mentor meetings. It is important to give a consistent message that meetings of the induction program take precedence when conflicts occur.

Engage the Staff

School leaders may want to use Spring faculty meetings to encourage staff to think about how the school will welcome next year's beginning teachers. In some schools, mentors draw on their experience with new teachers to design, with the mentor coordinator, the following year's plan. The following suggestions may work well in your school.

"I Remember"

Start a faculty meeting with "I Remember," a reflective activity you model with a partner first.

You and a partner stand in front of the staff. You say a sentence about something you remember from your first year of teaching.

> *"I remember how when I started I wanted to right all the wrongs that teachers had done to me as a student."*

Then your partner takes a turn.

> *"I remember how my first year I had no life...preparing lessons and correcting papers every night and weekends."*

Then you take another turn.

> *"I remember how Jason Bullworth locked the supply closet while I was inside and I couldn't figure out whether to yell bloody murder or wait a minute until another teacher came in for her supplies."*

You each take three turns, starting your one or two sentence remarks with "I remember..." The whole modeling takes about 2 minutes.

Ask the faculty to pair up with partners and simultaneously repeat what you modeled, speaking from their own recollections. Let the activity go on for about four minutes.

This activity provides a warm-up before you give a brief talk on how important it can be for new teachers to have people watching out for them and helping them along in the first year. You can ask for suggestions for how you and the staff can create conditions in which your beginning teachers can have a positive and supportive experience.

"I Wish I Knew Then"

- Ask each faculty member to write down seven things they wish they'd known when they started teaching their first year. Have everyone say one item out loud as you go around the room. Collect the lists and have them typed up, eliminating duplicate items. Pass them out at the next faculty meeting to kick off the continuing discussion of how everyone will take a part in supporting the new teachers.

- *Alternate version: Ask the staff to identify the things we veterans may take for granted that new teachers will need to know.*

Cards in a Basket

- Ask each faculty member to write on a card the best teaching tip they ever got. Ask them to sign the card. Collect the cards in a basket. Leave the basket in the teachers' lounge.

- Rule: anyone can look at the cards but you can't take a card away. If you read a card and it isn't clear to you what the person meant, ask them. Request they flesh out what they said on the card so that the beginning teacher who reads it next fall will know fully what they meant.

- The purpose of the activity is to make the cards maximally useful to the incoming beginning teachers. But there's a tacit agenda too. From the beginning, guess who wants to look over all those "best teaching tips?" Your veteran staff!

- This activity accomplishes two things. It gets your veteran staff learning from one another, talking to one another, and, because of the feedback and clarification process, makes the tips more understandable to a third party reader – such as the beginning teachers. This basket serves as a resource in future years, too, and can be supplemented annually.

Other Ideas

- Ask faculty members to write on a card some aspect of their teaching that they would be willing to share with, demonstrate, or teach to a beginning teacher. Post these cards in the teacher's lounge in the fall.

  Alternate version: Collect the cards into a document that is distributed to beginning teachers – and the rest of the faculty – in the fall.

- Encourage your faculty to share a practice, a strategy, or an element of a curriculum. A few teachers may think they have nothing special to offer; others may feel too busy. School leaders who have visited in classrooms will know from first hand observation the teacher's strengths. Poke your head in the door some afternoon of those people who don't reply the first time. *"Hi, Jane. Would you be willing sometime next fall to show one of our novices how you set up literature groups?"* The direct request may do the trick.

- During orientation in August, ask veteran teachers to share with beginning teachers samples of student work that show a before and after snapshot of what students can be expected to produce at the beginning and end of the year. Teachers can include writing samples, lab reports, social studies essays, or other items that are relevant to the class the beginning teacher will teach. These samples will give new teachers a concrete idea of their incoming students' skills and what gains they should shoot for (and can expect) over the course of the year.

- Ask the PTO president to arrange for someone to deliver a rose or goody basket to each beginning teacher at the end of the first day, along with "congratulations" for having gotten over the first big hurdle.

- Before school or in the early weeks of school, arrange for neighborhood parties, dinners, coffees, or other social events that help beginning teachers come to know community members and the parents of their children.

Supervision and Evaluation of Beginning Teachers

In a comprehensive induction program, it is expected that the mentor is in a non-judgmental and non-evaluative relationship with the beginning teacher. Further, the mentor does not play a role in the evaluation of the beginning teacher and does not participate in decision making on the future employment of the new teacher.

It is the role of the administrator to support, supervise, and evaluate beginning teachers. The skills, knowledge, and beliefs that the administrator brings to this role can be vital to the success, professional growth, and retention of the new teacher. We include the supervision and evaluation of the beginning teacher in the strategies for administrators because these functions are clearly an integral part of the program of support that surrounds and can make a difference in the effectiveness of a new teacher.

Supervision and Evaluation Systems

Supervision and evaluation systems in school districts transmit the culture of the district. They send messages of trust or mistrust, support or "gotcha." They may take the art and craft of teaching seriously or produce a set of superficial inspection procedures that indirectly show disrespect for teachers and teaching.

Evaluation systems need to be able to deal with unsatisfactory teaching in ways that are fair, direct, and decisive. At the same time, evaluation needs to be embedded in a larger program of support that emphasizes growth and professionalism. Jon Saphier (1993) and Andrew Platt (1999) describe ways to create a comprehensive supervision and evaluation system that is designed to deliberately strengthen school culture and professional community.

Suggestions for Supervisors

Supervisors should always keep high on the agenda the beginning teachers' belief systems, especially their beliefs about students' capacity to learn. It is the role of the supervisor, supported by new teachers' relationships with their mentors, to cultivate the desired *habits of mind* in the beginning teacher and to demonstrate that the beginning teacher must take responsibility for the learning of *all* students in the classroom. A supervisor can never neglect this issue, especially if there is evidence that the beginning teacher uses stereotypes in thinking about certain students or treats students differentially. If supervisors pick up "beliefs about children" as an issue when classroom management problems erupt, they are advised to "triage" the immediate problem - but make a note to raise the beliefs issue at another time.

Beginning teachers pose special challenges for supervisors such as principals, assistant principals, and department chairs. If, after a comprehensive classroom observation of a beginning teacher, the principal wrote down everything she saw that needed improvement, she could easily overwhelm and discourage the new teacher. In providing feedback, the supervisor is advised to be selective in providing feedback and to address "doable chunks." Supervisors are advised to guard against being pressed into completing lengthy, elaborate reports early in the new teacher's year. As the year progresses, however, it will be necessary for the evaluator to provide honest appraisals of the strengths and weaknesses of the new teacher so that appropriate rehiring decisions can be defended and understood.

Supervisors will want to be sensitive to the developmental needs of beginning teachers and look for ways to support them with their developmental growth. Typically (but not necessarily), beginning teachers have a lot to learn about classroom management, setting norms and routines, and dealing with disruptive behavior. At the same time, they may require support in planning lessons that are tightly aligned with curriculum objectives.

Consider the following progressive sequence of areas to which a supervisor may want the new teacher to pay attention:

• Classroom management

• Precision in lesson and unit planning for students' mastery thinking

• Multiple approaches to assessment that include continuous feedback to students

• A variety of instructional strategies

• Adjustment of instructional strategies that respect students' individual learning styles

• Advanced areas for teacher development:

  - Classroom climate

  - Models of teaching including cooperative learning

  - In-depth knowledge of specific pedagogies

Growth oriented supervision that nurtures beliefs that are essential to teaching all children and respects the developmental needs of new teachers will also result in supporting and retaining the teachers we want in our classrooms.

Component 7:
On-Going Assessment

Assessment of induction programs involves collecting a flow of information that enables the steering committee and others to monitor and improve the program. Induction program assessment should focus on the effectiveness of the program and never be confused with the assessment of the new teachers or the mentors.

Continuous Assessment

Evaluate the program, not the people.

An effective induction program takes its pulse throughout the year and in many different ways.

- Is the program useful for beginning teachers? Do they feel it is making a difference in their classroom teaching?

- What are the most useful forms of support for the second and third year teachers?

- Do the veteran teachers believe that the program is helping them to support the new teachers?

- How does the program contribute to improving student learning?

- How does the program support the professional growth of veteran teachers?

- What would be more useful approaches for making this program effective for new and veteran teachers?

- How is the induction program integrated with other programs that support the school or district as a learning community?

Quantitative and Qualitative Approaches

There are quantitative and qualitative ways to determine the impact that a comprehensive induction program is having on students and on staff.

Quantitative measures can provide important data about a program. Some of the data can be used for statistical analysis and other information will be useful in planning for future staff development for new teachers and mentors.

• How often are new and veteran teachers meeting in formal or informal conferences?

  • *How many informal and formal meetings did you and your mentor have this year?*

  • *How many times were you able to observe your mentor or another teacher?*

  • *How many times was your mentor a visitor in your classroom?*

• Who has been observing whom?

  • *Do you have the time and coverage you need to engage in classroom visitations or observations?*

  • *Is there conferencing before and after the visitations?*

• What is the district's experience with attracting teacher candidates? What is the district's success rate in hiring the teachers to whom it offers contracts? Has this rate changed since the induction program was instituted?

• What is the district's rate of retention of new teachers? How has retention changed since the induction program was instituted?

- What are the topics of the formal or informal conferences between mentors and protégés?

  - *Ask mentors for suggestions for topics for staff development for new teachers.*

    Mentors may note that new teachers are:

    - *Asking for clarity on the district curriculum*

    - *Seeking additional strategies for classroom management*

    - *Indicating discomfort with their relationships with parents*

    - *Evidencing high levels of stress*

  - *Does the frequency of certain topics that appear on the mentors' and new teachers' logs indicate that teachers need some training in these areas?*

- What is the attendance rate at the workshops or professional development activities that are offered by the district for mentors and protégés? How do the participants rate the usefulness of these sessions?

Principals or mentor coordinators find it useful to hold periodic meetings with the mentors and new teachers to provide information and training and to gather information on how well the program is meeting the new teachers' needs. Often these meetings are held in separate groups - mentors only or protégés only. Mentors or protégés may be invited to share information on topics that emerge in their discussions - with care taken by the mentors and the administrators to keep the conversations general and not linked to a specific teacher.

Qualitative approaches to evaluation can give a somewhat richer picture of the impact of the program. They can provide an indication of the affect that the program is having on new and veteran teachers and on the culture of the school or district.

- How do the beginning teacher and the mentor believe they have grown as a result of this program?

  - *Which aspects of your practice do you think were most influenced by the mentor program?*

  - *What did you find most/least satisfying about the program?*

  - *What further support for the program should come from the district? From the building principal?*

Program evaluation is best done when it becomes a routine aspect of on-going activities.

- Use five or ten minutes during networking meetings of mentors or beginning teachers to engage in formal or informal assessment of how the program is going.

- Ask mentors, new teachers, superintendents, other administrators, union leaders, and relevant others to fill out surveys at intervals throughout the year. (See Appendix E.)

- Seek feedback from the teachers association on its assessment of the program. Information that teachers give to the association may differ in instructive ways from information gathered by the administration.

Careful and candid evaluation of the data generated by new and veteran teachers is critical. It provides information on aspects of the program to be celebrated, ways in which the program can be strengthened, and suggestions for opportunities that can be realized.

Information from the evaluations should be shared with all constituencies who have a role in the success of beginning teachers. Using district and building newsletters, web sites, cable tv, and the local media, disseminate summary appraisals of your induction program to teachers, administrators, the school committee, parents, potential candidates, and all others whose support and involvement are critical to the success of the program.

Chapter Four

Maintaining and Sustaining Induction Programs

As districts hire increasing numbers of new teachers, it becomes critical that they incorporate the support of new teachers into their organizational structure. Most districts designate an administrator or teacher as the program coordinator who oversees the implementation of the induction program. The coordinator often has a multi-faceted role that includes:

- Collaborating with others to design and implement the district orientation program for new teachers

- Arranging for professional development activities for veteran teachers on their mentor role and for beginning teachers who are in their first three years of teaching

- Convening new teachers and mentors for informational and socializing meetings during the year

- Overseeing the collection of mentors'/protégés' meeting logs and other data on the induction program

- Reporting to the superintendent, other central office administrators, and the school committee on the program's successes and needs

- Providing mediation, and reassignment if needed, for beginning teacher-mentor pairs

Coordinators often establish steering committees that can serve as a sounding board for the coordinator and as "eyes and ears" for the program. Some steering committees are composed of a representative from each building while others include new and veteran teachers, building administrators and central office staff, and teacher association representatives. Steering committees help to monitor the development of programs, recommend training topics for new and veteran teachers, and encourage participation in the program.

Reward and Appreciate Mentors

To stipend or not to stipend is a question asked by many districts. It is our belief that mentors, who represent the most respected teachers in the schools, should be recognized for the important work they do in supporting new teachers. We recommend a 5% salary increment for mentors, but we also recognize that a lesser rate may be necessary for some districts. Mentor recognition can also take the form of compensatory time and a lesser stipend. In some districts, a menu of options is available, from which the mentor makes selections (see Appendix B). In determining their stipend policy, districts take into account system-wide precedents on how teachers are rewarded for work they do outside of the classroom as well as alternative recognition initiatives that may or may not involve financial remuneration.

The work of the mentor is not easily contained in neat blocks of time. For this reason, mentoring is not like coaching a team, advising a school club, or serving on a committee. While a minimum amount of time for conferencing and observations is usually specified, most mentors find that they spend substantially more time with their beginning teachers than the minimum that is suggested. For this reason, it is our experience that stipends should not be related to the time that is anticipated or to "hourly rates" that may be specified for other extracurricular work or in other contractual agreements.

In addition to providing compensation to mentors, districts can use a variety of ways to acknowledge the contributions of mentors:

- Reports to the school board on the induction program can include presentations by some of the mentors and their protégés.

- Newsletters to parents should introduce the mentors and explain their role in supporting the professional practice of new teachers.

- The parents' organization, the teachers union, or others can partner with the superintendent, principals, and the mentor coordinator in providing appreciation events such as coffees or luncheons during the school year.

- At faculty meetings, mentors can report on their involvement in the induction program and encourage other teachers to network with beginning teachers this year and become mentors next year.

Roadblocks for Induction Programs

When induction programs lose the support and respect of the staff, it is often for one of two reasons:

Breaches of confidentiality

A breach in the trust that all stakeholders have in the confidentiality of the program is likely to destroy the relationship between the mentor and the new teacher.

When principals seek to get information about new teachers from their mentors, confidentiality is breached. Similarly, when principals or other supervisors seek to give messages to new teachers through their mentors, confidentiality is breached.

In either case, if beginning teachers or their mentors sense in any way that the confidentiality of their relationship is endangered, the induction program will run into trouble. Principals and other administrators - as well as other teachers in the building, need to understand that the new teachers are valued professionals in the building and that they are to be treated with the same professional respect as other professionals in the school. Principals and supervisors must rely on their own first-hand sources of information on the professional performance of the new teacher - and not on data from the mentor.

Lack of equity

If decisions that surround the induction program do not impact all new teachers equally, the induction program will be at risk.

If beginning teachers have reason to believe that the induction program represents a way to provide "remediation" for new teachers, few new teachers will be willing to participate in the program.

Districts that are not able to provide a mentor for all of their new teachers are advised to identify criteria that will ensure that there is no tinge of remediation or any other form of stigma associated with decisions on which new teachers will have mentors. A district may decide to provide mentors only for novice teachers, and not for those who are new to the district but not new to the profession. If not all new teachers can be accommodated in workshops, districts may want to make workshops voluntary or establish criteria that explain which teachers are eligible to participate.

Respect the program and the participating teachers

Induction programs are complex and sensitive initiatives in any school district. They involve highly valued teachers in sharing their expertise and accumulated wisdom with the newest members of the school community. Induction programs provide these educational role models opportunities to carry forward into the future the treasury of knowledge, attitudes, and beliefs that have sustained them through their careers.

- Mentors will question school administrators about how truly they are valued if they are not given the time they need to do this important job effectively.

- If the induction program is perceived by staff as a way for administrators to shift their responsibilities for growth-oriented supervision to the mentor teachers, the program will lower morale in the schools.

Induction programs that demonstrate respect for veteran teachers can also be powerful vehicles for retaining these teachers. As research continues to demonstrate, the teachers who have been hired in the last 10 years are seeking to have a role in the decision making and management of their schools. They appreciate opportunities to engage in collegial relationships with other teachers that advance their own knowledge and skills. When district and school leaders make a commitment to ensuring that mentoring relationships are meaningful to the participants and valued by the district, they will find that the professionalism of the district improves as teachers make decisions about remaining in the district and in the profession.

CHAPTER FIVE

Beyond Mentoring: Induction and Professional Learning Communities

A Network of Learners

The Collegium Public School District hired 40 new teachers for 2005 -2006, 22 for the elementary schools and 18 who would be teaching in either the middle or high school. While the vast majority of these teachers were new to the profession, several had experience in other school districts.

In the initial interviews with applicants for the positions, the principals and superintendent emphasized the collegial culture that exists among the staff. They set out the expectation that new teachers will be participating members of the school's professional learning community. They described the many ways that teachers work together - as learners and as teachers - to strengthen the

continued...

continued from previous page...

learning experiences of all students in the school. They explained that the success of the students was a joint responsibility of the school staff. Equally, the success of the teachers was a joint responsibility that the staff took upon itself. Through study groups, co-teaching, informal peer observations, candid conversations about teaching, and frequent opportunities for reflection, new and veteran teachers were continually working together to strengthen the impact that they had on the children's learning and performance.

School and district leaders explained that at Collegium, new teacher induction is a fully integrated component of the district's professional learning community. New teachers are paired with highly qualified mentors who are appropriate in terms of their grade level and content area. The new teachers' classrooms are located near that of their mentors. From their first days at the school, the newcomers are members of a teaching and learning team in which new and veteran teachers provide feedback to each other, examine teaching practices, and partner in classroom teaching. The school bustles with a culture of continuous improvement: How could I have done this differently? What other approaches could I have used? How can I help you? The prevailing assumption among the staff is that no one has all of the answers and that together they can improve their collective ability to strengthen teaching and learning in the school.

Throughout the year, the principals sought feedback from new and veteran teachers on their experiences as members of the professional learning community. A sampling of this feedback provides a glimpse into the ways that the professional learning community supports new teachers.

Comments from New Teachers:

"From the beginning of the year, I felt like a member of a team. I was always working closely with other new and experienced teachers whom I could ask questions and who gave me great ideas."

"I learned so much from the other teachers - often without having to ask. In our team meetings, through co-teaching, and in everyday conversations, we talked about both the "nuts and bolts" of teaching as well as deeper issues about how children learn. It was so helpful and stimulating!"

"The environment at our school amazes me. Everyone is focused on how they can do something better and what more they can learn. People try out new ideas and share their results with each other, seeking feedback, suggestions, and other approaches. The air is alive with the electricity of the teachers."

Comments from Veteran Teachers:

"The new teachers are bringing wonderful, fresh thinking to our discussions. It is so useful when they question why we do something - and force us to reexamine. More than once, these questions have led us to examine practices that are helping to eliminate our achievement gaps."

"As a mentor, I find it very personally satisfying to work with my new teacher. I like the challenge of talking about my teaching - and of finding ways to

continued...

continued from previous page...

*support him as he grows as a confident teacher.
However, I could never, on my own, help him to
integrate into the school community as well as he has
if we did not have a strong learning community
here. Our network of professional colleagues greatly
enhances my ability to provide both professional and
personal support."*

*"The new teachers who have been joining our staff
in the last few years have made contributions from
their first days with us. They pick up easily on our
goal of open, honest communication and on the
importance of developing professional relationships at
the school. As we welcome new cohorts of teachers at
the school, we are strengthening the network of
learners here."*

Professional Learning Communities

Professional learning communities (PLCs) have been
described, over the past 15 years, as schools and districts in
which teachers and administrators are in a continuing quest to
expand their knowledge about teaching and their skills and
creativity in implementing effective practices. These
communities place a priority on enabling teachers and
administrators to assess the impact of their work with
children, collaborate on new approaches to teaching and
learning, and support each other with ongoing inquiry for
continuous improvement. PLCs provide teachers with training
on effective strategies for engaging in team discussions on

curriculum, instruction, and assessment. They encourage teacher leadership as cohorts of teachers explore current research and literature, share best practices, support and coach each other, and collaborate to strengthen the culture of the school as a learning environment.

The professional learning community in these schools presents an ideal environment for a new teacher. It provides a climate in which new and veteran teachers come together daily as learners who are intent on improving their professional practice in order to strengthen student learning in their school. The induction program becomes one with the professional learning community as it implements the four elements that distinguish a PLC:

- Shared responsibility by all teachers for the successful achievement of all students in the school

- Quality staff development that results in strengthening teaching, learning, and assessment

- Common commitment by the staff to develop a community of learners who are focused on continuous improvement of their knowledge and skills

- Seamless entry into the learning community for new and experienced teachers

In schools and districts that are implementing PLCs, mentors play a vital role in inducting new teachers into the culture and norms of the community. They provide an essential role as personal guide, confidante, trained observer, reflective practitioner, and "critical friend." They help to model the professional belief that the improvement of practice is a career-long journey best made in the company of colleagues (Lambert, 2003).

Multiplier Benefits

A well-design induction program is essentially excellent staff development.

The best part of being a mentor was having the opportunity to get new ideas from my beginning teacher. Sometimes it seemed that I learned as much from her as I was able to share with her.

Veteran mentor teacher

My mentor and I took a course on teaching in a standards based classroom that was helpful in giving us a way to talk with each other about our teaching. He told me that our discussions were as useful to him as I felt they were to me.

Beginning teacher

The activities that take place between the mentor and the protégé include the collegial behaviors that were identified by Judith Warren Little (1982) and Susan Rosenholtz (1982) as key to strengthening classroom practice.

COLLEGIALITY

A HIGH FREQUENCY OF TEACHERS **TALKING WITH EACH OTHER ABOUT TEACHING**

A HIGH FREQUENCY OF **TEACHERS OBSERVING EACH OTHER**

A HIGH FREQUENCY OF TEACHERS **PLANNING, MAKING, AND EVALUATING CURRICULUM MATERIALS** TOGETHER

A HIGH FREQUENCY OF TEACHERS **TEACHING EACH OTHER** ABOUT THE PRACTICE OF TEACHING

A HIGH FREQUENCY OF TEACHERS **ASKING FOR AND WILLING TO PROVIDE** ONE ANOTHER WITH **ASSISTANCE**

Judith Warren Little/ Susan Rosenholtz

When new and veteran teachers engage in "teacher talk," observe each other in the act of teaching, and participate in active inquiry on their practice, the children in their classrooms and schools benefit. Research continues to indicate that professional interactions that are embedded in the school - on the job - are the most effective in impacting classroom practice and student achievement. Newmann, Wehlage (1995), and others have found that students whose teachers have developed a true professional community show performance gains that are significantly greater than those of similar students in schools in which teachers are not engaged in collaborative learning. Based on this research, it is reasonable to assume that new teachers, who have high quality mentors and who participate in learning communities, are more likely to engage their students in learning and thinking that results in higher student achievement.

> **Effective induction programs that are integrated into the fabric of the professional learning community support the goal of transforming the culture of the school.**

All of the beginning teachers in the school were asked to identify practices they would like to observe in another teacher's classroom, such as the use of graphic organizers, a particular cooperative learning structure, or a use for PowerPoint presentations. Some of my colleagues and I asked if we could also have a chance to do some of these observations. The principal sent around a survey asking all teachers to identify two practices they would like to observe in another classroom and two practices they would be pleased to demonstrate to others. We used a faculty meeting to discuss how we would maximize the benefits of these observations by linking them to pre and post observation conversations on the practices being observed. These focused observations have changed many attitudes in our school! It is now common practice for teachers to share, observe, and learn from each other on a regular basis. As a result, I think we all are feeling that we are better teachers - and that our children are getting better teaching from us.

Veteran teacher

Induction programs build a comfort zone for new and veteran teachers as they engage in collegial behaviors, especially classroom observations. Veteran teachers report that they are more confident being observed teaching by a beginning teacher than by another veteran colleague. This comfort level increases - resulting in greater frequency of new and veteran teacher observations - as teachers gain experience in peer classroom visitations.

If there are six new teachers in a school this year and each is paired with a mentor with whom they engage in reciprocal observations, the school now has 12 teachers who are expanding their ability to engage in collegial practice. If next year, another six new teachers and six mentors are paired for similar practice, the number expands. After three or four years, it may be that every teacher in the school has participated in collegial conferencing and observing with a new or veteran colleague. The multiplier effect can be powerful - especially if teachers are given training, time, and support for these collegial interactions.

As veteran teachers work to support new teachers, an unexpected and powerful benefit can be the change that takes place in the culture of the school. All teachers become more open to experimentation. All teachers are willing to engage in open and honest communication about their practice, making teaching more productive for the students and rewarding for the teachers.

A Seamless Continuum

"Every Child Deserves an Expert Teacher Who..."

... can think and problem solve, based on an ever growing base of professional knowledge

... knows and cares about him or her personally

... works in a school district that knows and cares about every beginning teacher's growth toward real expertise!

We not only support the need for expert teachers, but believe it should be an urgent national policy. A democracy that claims every citizen can rise on his or her merit owes its children the chance to develop their minds and their possibilities. This opportunity does not take place for all youngsters today, especially economically disadvantaged youngsters whose education is hampered by poor or mediocre teaching. Further, we know that the cumulative effect of several poor teachers in a row creates damage that is extremely difficult to overcome later.

- A teacher who assembles a constellation of strategies and successfully overcomes the reading problems of several students now can tackle the "available issue" of critical reading with the same children.

- A teacher who overcomes discipline problems and becomes an accomplished classroom manager can take on the "available issue" of building a supportive, respectful community among the students.

These "available issues" emanate from inquiry and analysis. These teachers are always pushing their own envelope and identifying the next problem that will extend their practice further. These practices are the signs of an expert.

Comprehensive induction programs that are implemented in professional learning communities provide a seamless continuum of experiences that lead a person toward becoming an expert teacher. When comprehensive induction programs embed a comprehensive map of teaching knowledge and empowering beliefs about children's learning, they assist teachers in perceiving and defining the next level of problem solving - so they can become leading edge teachers.

Let us mobilize the knowledge and resources at our disposal to provide quality teaching for all our children. Let us provide educators with comprehensive induction systems that build powerful learning communities that support and retain expert teachers.

APPENDICES

APPENDIX A

Sample Comprehensive Induction Plan

IDEALTOWN Public Schools Plan
for the Comprehensive Induction of New Teachers

The Idealtown Public Schools are committed to the success of all members of our school community – students and teachers. In order to support the large number of new teachers we are bringing into our schools, we have developed this comprehensive induction program that engages new and veteran teachers in collegial, professional growth.

Mission Statement
for the Idealtown Public Schools Comprehensive Induction Program

The purpose of the Idealtown Public Schools induction program is to provide a supportive professional community for teachers who are new to our school district. As a result of this program, we will enhance the collegial environment in our schools and facilitate on-going professional growth for new and veteran teachers that results in effective teaching and enhanced student learning.

Induction Program Goals

1. *To integrate new teachers into the culture and climate of our schools and our school district*

2. *To assist beginning teachers to manage the challenges that are common to all new teachers*

3. *To enhance new and veteran teachers' personal and professional development through reflection on their practice and on student learning*

4. *To retain highly qualified teachers in our schools*

Acknowledgements

The Idealtown Public Schools appreciates the involvement of the following individuals in the development of this Plan:

Dr. Larry Finn	Superintendent, Idealtown Public Schools
Dr. Steven Brooks	Director of Curriculum
Ms. Margie Sanchez	Principal, Goldenrod School
Mr. Juan Martinez	Principal, Evergreen School
Ms. Genevieve Pierce	Teacher, Science, IHS Idealtown Teachers Association Representative
Mr. Kevin Ellis	Teacher, Woodland Elementary School
Ms. Stephanie Santos	Teacher, Evergreen Elementary School
Ms. Shelby Grace	Teacher, Idealtown Middle School
Mr. Joel Green	Teacher, Idealtown High School
Ms. Amanda Ansonia	Teacher, Idealtown Middle School

We would like to express our appreciation to Tanya Thomas for her assistance in facilitating the process that resulted in the development of this plan.

Other Options that Idealtown might have chosen...

- *Convene a steering committee to review the district's current program for supporting new teachers.*
- *Drawing on the model offered in this booklet, identify components of the existing program that need to be strengthened or added.*
- *Draft a proposed induction plan that is reviewed by the administration and the teachers union. Make changes as appropriate and present the plan to the school committee and the community.*

Communication Plan

The Idealtown Public Schools recognize that the Comprehensive Induction Program is a valuable asset of our school district. It helps to implement our district goal of ensuring that our schools provide a highly professional environment in which effective approaches to teaching and learning guide all work for students and teachers. It also helps to ensure that Idealtown is able to attract and retain the strongest teachers to teach the children in our schools.

In order to ensure that the school community is aware of the benefits and operations of the induction program, a communications plan has been developed to expand community awareness of the program. This plan includes three components:

WHO should know about our comprehensive induction program?

- Teachers and other staff in our schools
- Parents and parent organizations
- School councils and advisory groups
- School administrators
- Superintendent and central office staff
- School Committee
- Businesses in town, including realtors
- Local media
- Candidates for teaching positions
- Area colleges and universities
- The State Department of Education
- Recently retired teachers who may want to help with the mentoring program

continued...

WHAT should they know about our comprehensive induction program?

- The research and rationale for an induction program
- The benefits of the program for students and teachers
- The cost benefits for the district
- The demographics of teachers in Idealtown – and the numbers of new teachers we will be hiring
- The expectations for mentors and their protégés
- How the program works: time expectations; information sharing; personal and professional support
- The workshops and other training in which new and veteran teachers will participate
- The resources needed: time, training, coordination, and funding

WHAT vehicles should be used to inform the school community and the larger community about the program?

- District newsletters
- District brochures
- District cable TV programs
- District website
- Presentations at school committee meetings
- Principals' newsletters
- Back-to-school nights and other school events
- Special features in the local media

ROLES AND RESPONSIBILITIES

of key players in
the Idealtown Public Schools
Induction Program

Role of the Beginning Teacher

To become knowledgeable about, and to participate in, the Idealtown Public Schools Induction Program

To welcome informal support from mentors on a daily basis

To meet with the mentor for a total of approximately 2-3 hours per week in formal and informal interactions

To keep a log of weekly meetings and to maintain a reflective journal

To be open to feedback and to engage in the practice of reflective teaching

To participate in the professional learning community at the school

To maintain the confidentiality of the mentor-protégé relationship

To develop a professional development plan and strive to address three specific professional goals

To meet and conference regularly with other new teachers

To be open, candid, and willing to share and try new ideas

To be a good listener and be willing to "try again"

To participate in the district's on-going assessment of the induction program

Role of the Mentor Teacher

To become knowledgeable about, and to participate in, the Idealtown Public Schools Induction Program

To attend training on the roles and responsibilities of mentors

To recognize that mentoring is an ongoing commitment

To support the new teacher's entry into the school's professional learning community

To meet with the beginning teacher for 2-3 hours weekly in formal and informal interactions focused on personal, professional, and related issues

To be open to feedback and to engage in the practice of reflective teaching

To be willing to be observed by the beginning teacher

To be willing to observe and provide constructive feedback to the beginning teacher

To facilitate resource acquisition and open communication among the new teacher, other teachers, the principal, and other administrators

To offer support through active listening and by sharing experiences

To be a coach and a buddy, and to model professionalism

To maintain professional respect and confidentiality around the mentoring relationship

To attend networking and professional development meetings related to the induction program

To participate in all phases of an ongoing assessment of the induction program

Role of the Principals

To become knowledgeable about the induction program

To assign students to classrooms - and provide teaching schedules - that maximize beginning teachers' opportunities to be successful

To ensure that beginning teachers have adequate supplies and materials

To mobilize all staff to understand that they have a stake in the beginning teachers' success and are expected to find ways to contribute to that success

To respect the confidentiality of the mentor/new teacher relationship

To inform prospective teachers about the program and the expectation that, if hired, they will participate

To support and encourage eligible staff members to become mentors

To attend and participate in the induction program training for administrators

To inform faculty and parents about the program and its benefits

To coordinate an orientation program and other hospitality events for new teachers

To select mentors for new teachers from a pool of veteran teachers who have been trained as mentors

To make matches between mentors and new teachers, taking into consideration grade level, subject matter, proximity, and personal style

To build an active support team around beginning teachers

To facilitate the new teachers' participation in the school's professional learning community

To provide and protect mentor-protégé time for planning, observing, and conferencing

To serve as a mediator where necessary

To model professionalism and support for the program

To participate in all phases of an ongoing assessment of the induction program

Role of the Idealtown Teachers Association

To participate as a partner in the development and refinement of the Idealtown comprehensive induction plan and program

To become knowledgeable about the program and its components and to provide input into its ongoing improvement

To demonstrate union support for the induction program

To inform veteran teachers about the opportunity for mentoring and mentor training

To take a leadership role in advocating for new teachers within the Idealtown Public Schools

To support the incorporation of language into the contract that supports new teachers and their mentors

To provide sustained, positive, and informal communications about the induction program

To recognize the intangible benefits of a mentoring program such as increased community support for and understanding of the education profession

To participate in all phases of an ongoing assessment of the induction program

Role of the Superintendent and Central Office

To become knowledgeable about the induction program and its components and provide input into its ongoing improvement

To participate in the Idealtown Public Schools Induction Program through activities such as the orientation program

To provide funding to support the program

To provide for beginning teachers a packet of information about the community and the school district

To serve as a "cheerleader" for the program

To provide visible staff support and to promote the goals of the program

To provide financial support for training, time for mentors and protégés to meet, and other resources necessary for an effective program

To actively communicate with the administrative team regarding the program's progress and impact

To act as a liaison between the school committee and the community for the program

To serve as an advocate of the induction program to the wider community

To create a climate that encourages ongoing assessment and supports changes as necessary

To model the intrinsic belief that a strong induction program will have a significant positive impact on students

To assess effectiveness of the program through a cost benefit analysis that includes data on teacher retention and student achievement

Role of the School Committee

To welcome new teachers and demonstrate support for the program during the Idealtown Public School's orientation program

To provide a liaison for the induction program's steering committee

To provide financial support for the program

To adopt a policy that ensures a comprehensive induction program for new teachers

To act as community "cheerleaders" for the program by publicizing it and demonstrating the Committee's support

To facilitate contractual negotiations that will support the induction program

To participate in all phases of an ongoing assessment of the induction program

To assess the effectiveness of the program through a cost benefit analysis that includes data on teacher retention and student achievement

Role of Other Members of the School Faculty

To be welcoming and supportive of new faculty

To attend a workshop to learn about the induction program

To provide new teachers with information about formal and informal policies, curriculum and instruction, and resources

To encourage and support new teachers by:

- Being friendly

- Sharing supplies

- Sharing curriculum ideas

- Respecting confidentiality

- Sharing knowledge, skills and strategies

To provide a positive school climate that contributes to the success of all adults and students

To recognize the induction program as a component of the school's professional learning community

To involve new teachers in activities of the professional learning community

To read communications (newsletters, union information, newspaper articles, etc...) disseminated on the program

To share individual challenges with new teachers so they know they aren't alone

To consider being a mentor in future years

Role of the Program Coordinator

To become knowledgeable about the program and its components and provide input into its ongoing improvement

To participate in the planning of the new teacher orientation

To encourage teachers to participate as mentors

To plan monthly meetings on key topics for beginning teachers

To plan several meetings a year for mentors that include training and addressing issues raised by mentors

To coordinate and oversee professional development programs for beginning teachers, mentors, and administrators

To represent the induction program on the governance bodies that advance the district as a professional learning community

To chair meetings of the Induction Program Steering Committee

To oversee and facilitate the monitoring and implementation of the district's induction plan

To develop an annual program review that is based on data from the program and shared with the Program Steering Committee

To mediate mentor-protégé pairings if necessary

To apply for grants for induction programs and seek other sources of funding to supplement the line item in the budget

To direct the evaluation of the program throughout the year

To develop periodic reports on the program for the superintendent and the school committee

Governance of the Program

The program coordinator position carries with it a stipend and the reduction of 2/5 teaching load.

An induction program steering committee, composed of the program coordinator, superintendent or assistant superintendent, two principals, three veteran teachers and two second year teachers will provide guidance and feedback to the program coordinator.

The program steering committee will meet at least once a year for a program review that is based on data collected by the program coordinator. Following this review by the steering committee, a report is developed by the program coordinator and sent to the superintendent.

Other Options that Idealtown might have chosen...

In smaller districts, the responsibility of coordinating the Induction Program is given to an assistant superintendent or a school principal. In large districts, the coordinator role is a full time position.

The committee that develops the plan for the Induction Program may become the nucleus of the steering committee. The individuals who comprise the planning committee are often the same individuals who are interested in the ongoing success of the program.

Who is a New Teacher in Idealtown?

In the Idealtown Public Schools, a new teacher is any teacher who is new to the profession or new to the Idealtown Public Schools.

New teachers are paired with a mentor for one year.

Other Options that Idealtown might have chosen...

A new teacher might be defined as any teacher who is new to the district or new to a grade level or content area.

Teachers who are new to the profession or new to the district could be paired with a mentor for one to three years, with reduced requirements for the number of meetings that are held in each successive year.

Teachers who are new to the profession or new to the district could be paired with a different teacher for each of the three years of the mentor pairing program in order to provide them with a range of models of teaching.

Training and Networking for New Teachers

Training

New teachers in the Idealtown Public Schools are highly encouraged to participate in the *Teachers[21] Beginning Teacher Institute*, a 36-hour course which carries with it 4 optional graduate credits. This course is designed specifically to address the needs of new teachers in their first or second year of practice.

This course is given once during the year, starting in August. Two full days of the course take place in August. The additional 24 hours take place in 3 hour sessions after school and 6 hour sessions on occasional Saturdays. An announcement of this course is given to all new teachers when they are hired into the district.

New teachers are expected to participate in other professional development offered by the district or their school that addresses learning goals for the school.

Teachers in their second and third years of practice are expected to focus their training on their content area, content-specific pedagogy, and student assessment.

New Teacher Meetings

New teachers are expected to meet monthly as a group with the induction coordinator or his/her designee to share information, address issues, and provide feedback on the induction program.

Beginning Teacher Network

A Beginning Teacher Network is convened by a highly qualified lead teacher from within the district for the purpose of providing a small group of 4 – 6 new teachers with a supportive environment for addressing issues related to their classroom practice and professional relationships. This lead teacher is identified according to criteria that have been included in the teachers' contract that was ratified in 2004.

The Network meets 10 times in one-hour sessions during the school year. A brochure describing this program is available from the program coordinator.

Criteria and Expectations for Mentors in Idealtown

District-wide minimum criteria and expectations for mentors have been established for the Idealtown Public Schools Induction Program.

Criteria for Mentors:

- Teachers with professional status and at least 3 years of experience
- Skillful communicators who can adapt to different communication styles
- Teachers who are current on and implement the best educational practice and who are committed to constant learning about the art and craft of teaching
- Teachers who are committed to collegial practices and experimentation
- Teachers with a proven track record for successful classroom practice and for persevering and building confidence with resistant students
- Teachers who have completed a program of study in mentoring and supporting new teachers

Other Options that Idealtown might have chosen......

- *Able to commit the time that is required*
- *Demonstrates a broad repertoire of teaching skills and an understanding of the district's standards and expectations*
- *Possesses personal skills such as enthusiasm, commitment to teaching, and a demonstrated ability to work with peers*
- *Exhibits an understanding of the skills for effective conferencing and observation*
- *Agrees to participate in a training program for mentors*
- *Flexible and organized*
- *Possesses a sense of humor*
- *Demonstrates a commitment to personal professional development and an openness to new ideas and methodology*

Expectations for Mentors

- Mentors will be available approximately 3 hours per week to work with the new teacher
- Mentors will complete, in the first year, a 36-hour course in mentor skill training. The first 12 hours of this course will be completed prior to starting the mentoring relationship. In the second year, mentors will complete an additional 36-hours of advanced mentor training.
- Mentors will observe the new teacher or otherwise be present in the new teacher's classroom at least once weekly.
- Mentors will be relieved of certain duties and meetings to provide them with time to engage in the mentoring relationship.
- Mentors will meet two times a year as a group with the principal and program coordinator to problem solve and assess the effectiveness of the program.
- Mentors and protégé will maintain logs that document their time together for purposes of accountability. These logs will also include a one-word description of the topics discussed (classroom management; parent conferences; lesson planning; etc.).

Services for Mentors

Training

All mentors are required to take the Mentoring New Teachers 36-hour course during the first year that they are a mentor. The first 12 hours of the course should be taken prior to starting the mentoring relationship. In the second year, mentors will complete an additional 36-hours of Advanced Mentor Training.

Networking

All mentors will be expected to meet as a group with the principal and program coordinator three times during the year to share issues related to mentoring, engage in joint problem-solving, and provide feedback on the induction program.

Services for Administrators

All central office and building administrators will participate in an institute on comprehensive induction that provides information on the roles, responsibilities, and expectations of stakeholders in induction programs.

Administrators also participate in institutes that address the role of the supervisor in supporting, supervising, and evaluating beginning teachers. These institutes will also focus on building a growth-oriented professional learning community in the schools.

Program Evaluation

The district will engage in ongoing assessment of the program through the following vehicles:

Quantitative Data

The following data will be gathered on the program:

- Number of new teachers and mentors participating
- Mentor and protégé logs that document the time and the focus of conferences and observations
- Retention statistics on new and veteran teachers
- Professional development programs in which the new teacher participated
- Professional development programs in which the mentor participated
- Number of individuals who were offered contracts and who signed these contracts

Qualitative Data

The district and individual schools will use a variety of approaches for collecting qualitative data on the program:

- Mid-year and end of year attitudinal surveys
- Summative questionnaires after training and networking events
- Formal and informal data gathering from participants about the aspects of their practice that were impacted by the program
- Formal and informal data gathering on improving the program
- Implementation of the state Department of Education induction program survey at the end of the year

Data gathered on the program will be documented and reported to the superintendent, the school board, and the school community through the superintendent's newsletter. Data will be reviewed by the Induction Program Steering Committee. Recommendations and suggestions are welcome and will be considered as the program is refined.

SAMPLE FORMS

for the Idealtown Public Schools

SAMPLE A

Idealtown Public Schools

The Mentor Program

ALL teachers are invited to participate in the induction program for new teachers.

How do YOU get started?

1. Attend an orientation meeting that explains the program. These programs are held in the Spring of each year. (A flyer announcing the program is attached to this Plan.)

2. Complete the district application for mentoring that is attached to this plan.

3. To become a mentor, you must participate in training. Enroll for a 36-hour, 4 graduate credit course on Mentoring New Teachers. See your principal for details.

4. The matching of mentors with new teachers will be done by building principals.

5. The Steering Committee, composed of building principals, a union representative, the mentor coordinator, and new and veteran teachers, will provide leadership and direction to the program. This committee will also coordinate training and networking programs for beginning teachers.

6. The district seeks to establish a "mentor pool" that will give us a source of trained mentors who will be able to support the large number of new teachers – at all grade levels – that we expect in the next 5 years.

Other approaches that could be used:

Many administrators find that asking specific teachers to apply to become mentors is a useful and productive approach. Some teachers who would be excellent mentors do not recognize this potential in themselves or need some encouragement to step forward.

All interested teachers can be invited to participate in the mentor training with the understanding that:
   1. not all of them will be selected to be mentors
   2. participation does not obligate them to become mentors

If application procedures do not produce sufficient mentor candidates, principals will select the veteran teachers whom they would like to be mentors of the new teachers. These selections will be based in part on their knowledge of the teachers whom they have hired for the new school year as well as the criteria of grade level, content area, and proximity in the building. Principals will work to arrange the mentor/protégé teachers' schedules to provide common meeting time and opposing times for classroom observations.

SAMPLE B
Idealtown Public Schools

Announcing the Idealtown Public Schools Mentor Program for New Teachers

Join your colleagues for an informational meeting on becoming a mentor teacher
DATE – TIME
LOCATION

Next year, 41 new teachers will be joining our staff. Because this is a record number of new teachers for any one year – and we can anticipate that we will be hiring numbers of new teachers in each of the next 3-5 years, the district has developed a Comprehensive Induction Program to support teachers new to Idealtown.

We would like YOU to consider being a mentor to a new teacher.
Mentoring is a wonderful way for you to share your wisdom and expertise, learn new ideas and strategies from a new teacher, and give back to your profession.

Criteria for Mentor Teachers
- Professional status and at least 3 years of experience
- Skillful communicators who can adapt to different communication styles
- Knowledgeable on and skilled with effective educational practices
- Committed to constant learning about the art and craft of teaching
- Committed to collegial practices and experimentation
- A proven track record for successful classroom practice
- Evidence of persevering and building confidence with resistant students
- Completion of a program of study in mentoring and supporting new teachers

Mentor Matching
Mentors will be matched with new teachers based on grade level, content area, and proximity in their buildings.

Requirements
- Willingness to be available to a beginning teacher for approximately 2-3 hours per week
- Willingness to observe a beginning teacher 3 times and to be observed 3 times, with accompanying pre and post conferences

Stipend: $ plus   Professional Development Points

RSVP:

SAMPLE C
Idealtown Public Schools

Mentor Application and Matching Form

Part A: Mentor Teacher Application

I am interested in being considered as a mentor for a new teacher in the comprehensive induction program. I understand that the role of a mentor is critical to the success of a novice teacher and ultimately key to the success of the children of Idealtown.

Name: _____

1. What specific personal and professional qualities would you bring to mentoring a new teacher?

   _____

   _____

   _____

   _____

   _____

   _____

   _____

2. How are you keeping current with your own professional development?
   What steps are you taking to be up-to-date on issues of curriculum and assessment?

   _____

   _____

   _____

   _____

   _____

   _____

   _____

continued...

3. What do you hope to gain from becoming a mentor?

_____

_____

_____

_____

_____

_____

_____

Signature: _____ **Date:** _____

Part B: For Office Use Only

Selection Committee's comments:

_____

_____

_____

_____

_____

_____

_____

Part C: Principal's Mentor – New Teacher Match

School: _____

Principal's Name: _____

I have selected **(name of mentor)** _____

who currently holds the position of **(grade and subject)** _____

to serve as a mentor teacher for **(name of new teacher)** _____

who has been appointed to the position of **(grade and subject)** _____

Principal's Signature: _____ **Date:** _____

SAMPLE D

Idealtown Public Schools

Application for the Position of Mentor of a New Teacher

Name: _____

School: _____

Department/Grade: _____

Years in the Idealtown Public Schools:

_____

Areas of Certification: _____

_____

Please write a statement about your interest in becoming a mentor and how you think you can assist a first year teacher in our district.

_____

_____

_____

_____

_____

_____

_____

I understand that I will be required to participate in a 36-hour mentor training course if I am chosen as a mentor. The first 12 hours must be completed before my work as a mentor begins.

Signed: _____   Date: _____

APPENDIX B

Ideas for Providing Reward and Recognition for Mentors

Ideas for Providing Reward and Recognition for Mentors

- Stipends
- Professional Development Points
- **Time** to work with beginning teachers
    - Extra preparation periods
    - Release from duties
    - Reduced teaching load
- Professional development opportunities
- Credit mentor experience toward step/lane advancement
- Increased classroom supply budget
- Training on being a mentor
- Skill training for working with protégés
- Recognition ceremonies
- Articles spotlighting mentors
- Mentor support groups
- Opportunities to take courses
- Vouchers
- Tuition reimbursement

Intrinsic rewards

- Opportunity to help a beginning teacher
- Opportunity to improve own teaching

Suggested guidelines for teachers' contracts: Include funds for providing stipends to mentor teachers. Most districts do not include stipends for beginning teachers.

APPENDIX C

Sample Induction Program Calendar

Sample Induction Program Calender

August 28	Orientation and reception for new teachers
	Training for new mentors
August 29	Mentors meet with new teachers in new teachers' classrooms
September	Mentors meet with new teachers at least twice weekly; daily if possible
Septmber 5	First day of school
September 26	Back to school night
September 30	New teacher meeting with coordinator or principal
October	Mentors meet with new teachers at least twice weekly; daily if possible
	New teacher/mentor classroom visitation
October 19	New teacher meeting with coordinator or principal
October 24	Parent Conferences start
October 26	First marking period ends
	Report cards due in the office on October 31
November	Mentors meet with new teachers at least twice weekly; daily if possible
	New teacher/mentor classroom visitation
November 6	Math night at school
November 14	Mentor meeting with mentor coordinator
November 21	Thanksgiving vacation starts
December	Mentors meet with new teachers at least twice weekly
December 12	New teacher meeting with coordinator or principal
December 19	Holiday celebration for parents and students
December 23	Holiday Vacation starts
	Mentor/new teacher logs due at the office

January	Mentors meet with new teachers at least once weekly
	New teacher/mentor classroom visitation
January 2	Holiday vacation ends
January 18	Second marking period ends
February	Mentors meet with new teachers at least once weekly
February 7	Science night at school
February 12	Mentor Meeting with mentor coordinator
February 17	Winter Vacation starts
February 24	Winter Vacation ends
March	Mentors meet with teachers at least once weekly
	New teacher/mentor classroom visitation
March 14	New teacher meeting with coordinator or principal
March 29	Third period ends
April	Mentors meet with new teachers at least once weekly
April 13	Spring Vacation starts
April 21	Spring Vacation ends
May	Mentors meet with new teachers at least once weekly
May 3	Mentor meeting with mentor coordinator
May 5	New teacher meeting with coordinator or principal
May 10	State testing starts
May 24	Portfolio celebrations begin
June	Mentors meet with new teachers at least once weekly
June 14	Fourth period ends
	Report cards due in the office on June 19
June 21	Last day of school
	Mentor/new teacher logs due at the office

Appendix D

Self-Assessment Tool for School Districts

Self-Assessment Tool for School Districts

This survey is designed to give union and school leaders an opportunity to reflect on the areas in which their district is incorporating the elements of a comprehensive induction program.

Place an "X" in the box that is appropriate for each item.	YES	NO	Partially
District-wide Planning Process			
Has our district engaged a broadly based group of teachers and administrators in the process of developing a plan for the district's induction program? Does this group include the teachers' union and the school administration?			
Does a district-wide steering committee monitor the implementation of the program and use feedback to adjust and improve it?			
Is the induction program part of the district professional development plan?			
Is the induction program integrated into school and district programs for building a professional learning community?			
Criteria-based Selection and Matching of Mentors			
Does our district have criteria or qualifications for the selection of mentors?			
Are mentors selected based on the criteria that have been established by the district?			
Does our district have criteria for the matching of mentors and protégés?			
Are the matches between mentors and protégés made based on criteria established by the district?			
Mentor Services			
Do mentors receive training in the skills of providing positive feedback and differential conferencing before being paired with beginning teachers?			
Do mentors receive training in the skills of providing support for beginning teachers in the areas of curriculum, instruction, and assessment?			
Is there a specified expectation regarding the frequency of interactions (conferences, observations) between the mentor and the protégé?			

Place an "X" in the box that is appropriate for each item.	YES	NO	Partially
Beginning Teacher Services			
Do the beginning teachers in the district participate in workshops (on topics such as classroom management, building a classroom culture, working with families, etc.) that are specifically tailored to the needs of beginning teachers?			
Are beginning teachers brought together in networking groups regularly during the year?			
Are beginning teachers given support to observe their mentors and other colleagues?			
Are beginning teachers given opportunities to be observed by and get productive feedback from their mentor or other new or veteran colleagues?			
Principal Services			
Do principals model for their staff a range of ways to support new teachers?			
Do principals use a wide range of approaches to enlist all staff in the support of new teachers?			
Do principals use supervision and evaluation for new teachers as a growth-oriented experience?			
School Board and Community			
Do the school committee and parents know that there is a comprehensive induction program in the schools? Do they understand that it is focused on supporting the professional growth of new and veteran teachers?			
Is the community invited to contribute to district efforts to support beginning teachers?			
On-going Assessment			
Does the district-wide steering committee engage in on-going assessment of the induction program?			
Does the district-wide steering committee gather summative information on the impact of the induction program? Is this information shared with staff and the larger community?			

APPENDIX E

Sample Surveys for Beginning Teachers and Mentors

Informal Survey for Beginning Teachers

*For distribution at beginning teacher networking meetings
or training events*

1. What are the three most useful aspects of support that the district offers beginning teachers?

_____
_____
_____
_____
_____

2. What are the least useful aspects of the induction program?

_____
_____
_____
_____
_____

3. What recommendations do you have for our comprehensive induction program?

_____
_____
_____
_____
_____

Informal Survey for Mentors

*For distribution at mentor networking meetings
or training events*

1. What aspects of our mentoring program are the most useful to you – and to your beginning teacher?

_____

_____

_____

_____

_____

_____

2. From your point of view as a mentor, what are the least useful aspects of the induction program?

_____

_____

_____

_____

_____

_____

3. What recommendations do you have for our comprehensive induction program?

_____

_____

_____

_____

_____

APPENDIX F

The Knowledge Base on Teaching

Six Knowledge Bases of Professional Teaching

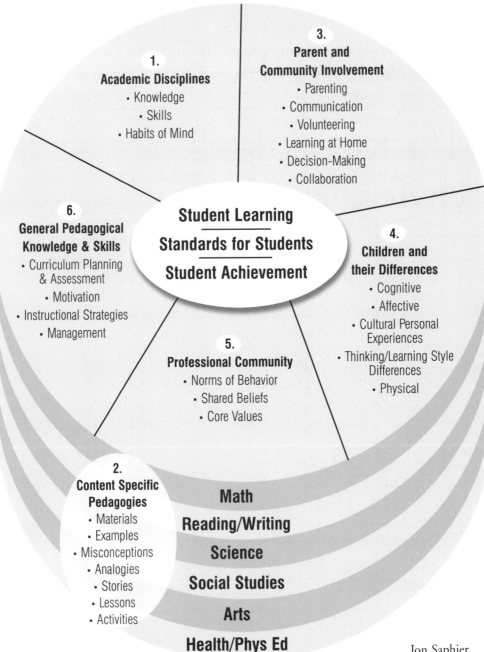

Student Learning
Standards for Students
Student Achievement

1.
Academic Disciplines
• Knowledge
• Skills
• Habits of Mind

3.
Parent and Community Involvement
• Parenting
• Communication
• Volunteering
• Learning at Home
• Decision-Making
• Collaboration

6.
General Pedagogical Knowledge & Skills
• Curriculum Planning & Assessment
• Motivation
• Instructional Strategies
• Management

4.
Children and their Differences
• Cognitive
• Affective
• Cultural Personal Experiences
• Thinking/Learning Style Differences
• Physical

5.
Professional Community
• Norms of Behavior
• Shared Beliefs
• Core Values

2.
Content Specific Pedagogies
• Materials
• Examples
• Misconceptions
• Analogies
• Stories
• Lessons
• Activities

Math
Reading/Writing
Science
Social Studies
Arts
Health/Phys Ed

Jon Saphier

Every true profession has a shared knowledge base that grounds its practice. A knowledge base is a set of ideas and concepts essential to high level practice. Every licensed professional is expected to have a working knowledge of these ideas and concepts. In a true profession, a common language and concept system evolves; words are developed to hold the complex meanings of important ideas. This common language facilitates communication; it empowers professional talk among practitioners as they consult and problem-solve with one another.

Obstructing the development of professionalism in teaching is the widespread belief that we do not have a knowledge base on teaching; that good teaching is an innate endowment. Worse is the parallel belief that teaching is relatively simple work and that good teaching comes only from teachers studying content in greater depth. This belief holds that good pedagogy requires only the acquisition of some simple management and organization strategies. **The truth is that teaching is intellectually complex, difficult, and demanding work grounded in a huge and sophisticated knowledge base that, if properly conceived, provides endless ground for study and personal growth.** Without the proper constructs for this knowledge base, true collegiality and experimentation are undercut.

We believe that acknowledging the professional knowledge base on teaching leads to the parallel development of a language and concept system that becomes a cornerstone of teacher learning.

A "knowledge base" has some important characteristics:

1. It is *organized*. It has certain categories and classifications for the areas acknowledged to be important.

2. It is *reliable*. We can count on the information it presents because its credibility has been established over time; this information is supported by practice and research.

3. It is *adaptable*. It is capable of assimilating new discoveries into its categories or changing the categories if this is warranted by new information.

A knowledge base forms the accumulated foundation of educational practice and gives education professionals a claim to public trust. Being decent and literate are not sufficient qualifications for becoming a member of a knowledge-based profession. The requisite knowledge and skill for teaching cannot be learned casually "on the job."

The Nature of Professional Knowledge

Policy makers operate from a wrong and oversimplified model of the knowledge base on teaching. This wrong model has enormous consequences for the structure of schools, for teacher learning, and for induction programs. These consequences inevitably curb reflection and invention. They result in widespread mediocrity among teachers. The image of teaching in this model starts a chain of actions that lead to treating teachers as low level functionaries whose job it is to "implement" curriculum and instruction - not to think about curriculum and instruction. This model is the "effectiveness" paradigm that assumes that there is a list of "effective" behaviors that can be identified, learned, and practiced to proficiency.

In any true profession, the nature of professional knowledge is quite different. It is built around three key concepts: 1) areas of performance, 2) repertoire, and 3) matching.

1) Areas of Performance

There are certain zones of work, or areas in which professionals are asked to operate:

- In law...
  One must have competence at writing briefs, taking depositions, filing motions, and preparing courtroom strategies.

- In architecture...
  One is called upon for drafting, choosing specifications for beams and trusses, picking an architectural style, interviewing clients to find out what they want, and making presentations to variance boards for exemptions from local regulations.

2) Repertoire

For each of these areas of performance there is *no one best way of handling the tasks.*

- In law...
  - no single best style for writing a brief
  - no single best courtroom strategy

- In architecture...
  - no one best specification for a main beam
  - no one best way to be persuasive with the zoning board

A *repertoire* of ways exists to accomplish any task, and no one approach is inherently better than any other. Queen Ann Victorian homes may be a better match to the tastes of the clients and to the neighborhood than Frank Lloyd Wright modern. Being scientific and precise in pointing out environmental benefits for a project may not be as persuasive with a given zoning board as showing personal concern for the elderly and the needs of the community. Good architects draw from a repertoire of options in order to meet the needs of the situation or the client.

3) Matching

In each case, professionals draw from their repertoire the responses that best suit or match the situation. The courtroom strategy is matched to the nature of the case and what is known about the personality of the judge. The design of the house is matched to the contour of the land and to the needs and desires of the owner. The architect is able to bring different house designs and different approaches to each individual case.

These three concepts are defining attributes of professional knowledge in *any* field. Professionals are decision-makers; they make decisions from an acquired and ever expanding repertoire. The responses they choose are the ones that are most appropriate to a given situation.

Similarly, in teaching there are many areas of performance. They occur in at least **six domains**, each of which bears directly on student learning.

Domain 1:
Academic Disciplines

Deep Knowledge, Skills, Habits of Mind

Teachers of chemistry must continue to expand and deepen their own knowledge of their subject. This study not only enables them to bring the latest and best knowledge to their students, it keeps teachers personally revitalized. It allows them to model meaningfully for their students what it means to be a learner. The same can be said for teachers in any discipline.

In the elementary levels, teachers need to understand at a deep level certain concepts that are embedded in their curricula. For example, the true nature of a "variable" in science is minimally understood by a large portion of elementary teachers. These teachers consider themselves "not scientists," yet are responsible for teaching science to their students.

Liping Ma's groundbreaking book, *Knowing and Teaching Elementary Mathematics* (1999), describes in detail the difference in teaching practice and student understanding that results when teachers have what she calls "Profound Understanding of Fundamental Mathematics:"

> *"Based on my research, I define understanding a topic with depth as connecting it with more conceptually powerful ideas of the subject. The closer an idea is to the structure of the discipline, the more powerful it will be. Consequently, the more topics it will be able to support...Depth and*

> *breadth…depend on thoroughness – the capacity to*
> *'pass through' all parts of the field – to weave them together.*
> *Indeed, it is this thoroughness which 'glues' knowledge*
> *of mathematics into a coherent whole."*

Deep content knowledge, particularly for elementary teachers, enables them to represent concepts in multiple ways and to tie the concepts together in true teaching for understanding. This deep understanding, perhaps more than any factor, accounts for the differences in mathematics and science instruction noted by Stigler and Heibert (1999) in the TIMMS studies and in their book, *The Teaching Gap*.

In addition to the concepts and skills of the discipline, the thinking skills and habits of mind associated with proficiency in the discipline are essential foundations for good teaching. Costa and Kallick, in *Habits of Mind* (2000), thoroughly profile these skills and their implications for teaching.

A necessary and on-going part of the continuing education of all teachers is studying the content they teach. This study must be accommodated in the design of professional development programs for teachers from initial certification through advanced professional career status.

Domain 2:
Content Specific Pedagogy

Stories, Analogies, Examples, Misconceptions, Materials, Activities

> *For second graders, there is a particular way to use orange and white Cuisenaire rods to illustrate place value; furthermore, there are a set of progressive games for them to play with those materials that are very effective in helping youngsters acquire a deep understanding of place values and fluency with the notation.*

> *At fifth grade, there is a set of practices and procedures that are very effective in helping youngsters learn to develop skills for doing peer editing conferences with each other.*

> *For middle school students, there is a very useful set of materials, distributed in 1987 by The Regional Math Network, that has realistic word problems that connect with adolescents' interests. Twenty years later, it is still powerful, but rarely circulated.*

The knowledge described above relates to a highly specific knowledge that teachers accumulate over their careers – knowledge of particular materials, instructional strategies, and procedures for teaching specific content. Learning these specific methods and materials and how to use them must be a part of the ongoing education of professional teachers, whether beginners or veterans. There is a large repertoire for each concept and skill. Expertise consists of making choices from content specific pedagogy that match with individual students and situations.

The knowledge base includes the wealth of good examples and analogies that can be used to teach particular concepts (e.g. the mailman delivering a bill as an analogy for negative numbers). In addition, teachers need to be able to identify common misconceptions that students are liable to bring to instruction (e.g. all rivers flow north to south) so they can be surfaced, contradicted, and replaced with new, accurate conceptions.

Opportunities to learn this knowledge must be built systematically into both beginning and continuing teacher education. Excellent collections of materials for teaching and assessing specific concepts and skills are available on teacher-oriented websites. The skill of being able to design such units and assessments, however, is generic, and is discussed in Domain 6, Generic Pedagogical Knowledge and Skills.

Domain 3:
Parent and Community Involvement

Parenting, Communication, Volunteering,
Learning at Home, Decision-Making, Collaboration

Joyce Epstein (1995), Anne Henderson, Karen Mapp (2002) and others have profiled the knowledge base on parent and community involvement and its impact on student learning. They have pointed out the importance of making school a welcoming place for parents. They have researched the role of parent ownership in school governance and change.

Teachers as well as administrators need to know and use the skills of parent involvement. One of these skills, communication with parents, can make a significant difference for students. Parents impact student acheivement when they communicate to their children that they believe education is important and that they can do well if they work hard and use good strategies. Teachers need techniques for augmenting parents' ability to reinforce the message that working hard is the way to achieve success at school. Teacher education in the 21st century needs to include knowledge and skill training in reaching out to parents and finding ways to involve them constructively in the life of the school and in the education of their own youngsters.

Domain 4:
Children and Their Differences

Developmental Physical, Cultural and Personal Experiences, Thinking/Learning Style Differences

Understanding and adjusting for differences in learners calls for the highest level of artistry from teachers as they draw on the repertoire they have developed in the other strands to optimize learning environments for students. It is in this domain that the all important issues of child development are addressed, including cognitive and emotional development. This knowledge is essential to good "matching" as teachers make selections from their own teaching repertoire.

There are other differences that are also important for teachers to understand.

- Differences in learning style, including perceptual preferences and the ways individuals process information. Teacher training should include a thorough understanding of the research on learning styles and the processes of the brain. Teachers should develop skills in adjusting their teaching styles to enhance students' learning rate and retention.

- Cultural differences among youngsters of different ethnic and regional heritages. The cultural backgrounds of children's homes can have significant impact on the attitudes and approaches youngsters bring to school. Teachers need to bring an understanding of these differences to their instruction.

- Students' race, color, and country of origin can influence their self-concept as learners, their attitudes about school, and their approaches to others who are different from themselves.

As we become a nation in which minorities are the majority, it is crucial that teachers help students to cultivate appreciation for their differences. Good teacher preparation educates teachers about these differences and how to help students view themselves and their classmates positively.

Domain 5:
Professional Learning Community

Cultural Norms, Shared Beliefs, Common Goals

All staff must understand the values, beliefs, and behaviors that are inherent in professional learning communities. They need to develop skills that support and nurture collegial growth such as reflective practice and inquiry; open, honest communication; collective creativity; and shared instructional leadership. Teachers and administrators have roles to play in developing a community of professionals who are invested in each others' growth and learning with the end-product of improving student learning. The school as a whole is a system that has a strong impact on the learning of the child; as members of a professional learning community, teachers have an impact on how well that system serves learning and growing in children.

Training for teachers helps them to understand key aspects of the professional learning community: cultural norms, common goals, and shared beliefs. A map of this knowledge base can be found in Figures 3 and 4.

Defining Professional Community for Increasing Student Achievement

Cultural Norms	+	Common Goals	+	Shared Beliefs	=	Professional Community

Cultural Norms

Ten norms for a culture of continuous improvement of practice

(see Figure 4)

Common Goals

1. Common proficiency targets for students with exemplars, aligned curriculum and assessments

2. Common staff development focus within schools based on analysis of student needs

3. Core values

Shared Beliefs

1. All students have the intellectual capacity to do quality work at high standards.

Effective effort is the key, not speed.

2. There is a real and complex Knowledge Base about Teaching

3. Shared responsibility: "All students belong to us."

4. "Our school can do a lot better for most of its students than we are doing now. Each child can succeed at important academic tasks every day."

Schlechty, P. *Shaking Up the Schoolhouse*, San Francisco: Jossey Bass, 2001, p.169

Provides energy for continuous improvement and trust in leaders

Provides direction & focus for the energy

Provides commitment to students and motivation to stay the course

Figure 3.

Ten Cultural Norms of Professional Community

The D.N.A... Requisite norms that allow all the others to develop	What "collaboration" really means: norms which result directly in improved instruction and better student achievement	Important background norms that generate affiliation and commitment
	3 Non-Defensive Self-Examination of Teaching Practice	**7** Protecting What's Important
1 Honest, Open Communication	**4** Systematic Examination of Data	**8** Appreciation & Recognition
2 Involvement in Decision-Making	**5** Reaching Out to the Knowledge Base	**9** Celebration, Caring, Humor, Traditions, Rituals, Ceremonies
	6 Experimentation, Analysis & Self-Critique in Groups	**10** High Expectations & Accountability for Adults
	Groups of teachers who share students and/or content demonstrate these behaviors in their meetings.	

Figure 4.

Domain 6:
Generic Pedagogical Knowledge

Management, Motivation, Instructional Strategies,
Curriculum Planning & Assessment

It is a paradox that the knowledge base on pedagogy is enormous, complex, rich, subtle, and vital to successful teaching – and yet it is barely present in teacher education. In fact, its very existence is sometimes denied.

The knowledge base on generic pedagogy is clear and explicit. It can be understood, like any professional knowledge base, in terms of useful categories that describe areas of teaching performance: Motivation, Management, Instructional Strategies, and Curriculum and Assessment Planning. It is essential that all professional teachers show high levels of competence in these areas if we are to educate all of our children to 21st century standards. Each area contains repertoires of very specific behaviors and patterns of thought that can be learned, practiced, and applied. When added together, they comprise the tools of highly complex knowledge that gets implemented through analysis, problem solving, and matching. Matching is the capacity to draw from one's repertoire a response that is appropriate to the situation. This knowledge base has been validated empirically and is a convenient lens for viewing the range and complexity of interactive teaching. (Saphier, 1997)

Knowledge of Motivation is used by teachers to influence students' desire to learn and their belief that it is worthwhile to do so. Teachers use motivation strategies to convince students that they have the capacity to succeed with challenging material. Using their knowledge of motivation, teachers develop skills for making students feel significant and capable.

Knowledge of Management is about enabling students to attain and sustain success with academic tasks. It refers to the teachers' skills in anticipating and removing obstacles to students' success.

Knowledge of Instructional Strategies describes the process of mastering powerful cognitive tools for helping students construct knowledge, anchor their learning, and connect learning to their lives.

Knowledge of Curriculum and Assessment Planning refers to the importance of developing teachers' capacity to be rigorous and complex curriculum thinkers. Teachers need to design experiences that have continuity, appropriate sequencing, and integration with other disciplines so that students understand these learning experiences as relevant to life and connected to other fields of knowledge.

BIBLIOGRAPHY

American Federation of Teachers. (2001). Educational Issues Policy Brief. *Beginning Teacher Induction: The essential bridge.* AFT: Washington, D.C.

Astuto, T.A., Clark, D.L., Read, A-M., McGree, K. & Fernandez, L. deK.P. (1993). *Challenges to dominant assumptions controlling educational reform.* Andover, Massachusetts: Regional Laboratory for the Educational Improvement of the Northeast and Islands

Bartell, C., & Ownby, L. (1994). *Report on the Implementation of the Beginning Teacher Support and Assessment Program,* 1992-1994. Sacramento, CA: California Commission on New Teacher Credentialing and California Department of Education.

Bereiter, C. and Scardamalia, M. (1993). *Surpassing Ourselves – An Inquiry into the Nature and Implications of Expertise.* Chicago: Open Court.

Berliner, D. (1987). "Ways of Thinking about Students and Classrooms by More and Less Experienced Teachers," in J. Calderhead (ed.), *Exploring Teachers' Thinking.* London: Cassell.

Comer, J. (1988). "Educating Poor Minority Children." *Scientific American.* 259:42-48.

Costa, A. L. and Garmston, R. J. (1994). *Cognitive Coaching: A Foundation for Renaissance Schools.* Norwood, MA: Christopher Gordon.

Costa, A. L. and Kallick, B. (2000). *Discovering and Exploring Habits of Mind.* Alexandria, VA: Association for Supervision and Curriculum Development.

Costa, A. L. and Kallick, B. (2000). *Activating and Enjoying Habits of Mind* (Habits of Mind, Book 2). Alexandria, VA: Association for Supervision and Curriculum Development.

Costa, A. L. and Kallick, B. (2000). *Assessing and Reporting on Habits of Mind* (Habits of Mind, Book 3). Alexandria, VA: Association for Supervision and Curriculum Development.

Costa, A. L. and Kallick, B. (2000). *Integrating and Sustaining Habits of Mind* (Habits of Mind, Book 4). Alexandria, VA: Association for Supervision and Curriculum Development.

Darling-Hammond, L. (1996). *What Matters Most: Teaching for America's Future.* New York: National Commission on Teaching and America's Future.

Darling-Hammond, L. (1997). *Doing What Matters Most: Investing in Quality Teaching.* New York: National Commission on Teaching and America's Future.

Darling-Hammond, L. (2000). *Solving the Dilemmas of Teacher Supply and Quality.* New York: National Commission on Teaching and America's Future.

Darling-Hammond, L. (2001). "The Challenge of Staffing Our Schools." *Educational Leadership.* 58(8), 12-17. Alexandria, VA: Association for Supervision and Curriculum Development.

Darling-Hammond, L.. & Sykes, G. (2003, September 17). Wanted: A National Teacher Supply Policy for Education: The right way to meet the "highly qualified teacher" challenge. *Education Policy Analysis Archives, 11(33).* Retrieved from http://epaa.asu.edu/epaa/v11n33/.

Dreyfus, H. L. and Dreyfus, S. E. (1986). *Mind over Machine.* New York: Free Press.

Educational Leadership. (May, 2001). This issue is devoted to "Who is Teaching our Children?" Volume 58, Number 8.

Edwards, J. (1994). "Thinking, Education and Human Potential." In J. Edwards, (ed.), *Thinking: International Interdisciplinary Perspectives.* Melbourne: Hawker Brownlow Education.

Epstein, J. L. (1995). "School/Family/Community Partnerships." *Phi Delta Kappan.* May, 1995.

Feiman-Nemser, S. & Parker, M. (1993). "Mentoring in Context: A Comparison of Two U.S. Programs for Beginning Teachers." *International Journal of Educational Research,* 19(8), 699-718.

Fideler, E. & Haselkorn, D. (2000). *Learning the Ropes: Urban Teacher Induction Programs and Practices in the United States.* Belmont, MA: Recruiting New Teachers, Inc.

Glickman, C. (2000). *SuperVision and Instructional Leadership: A Developmental Approach.* Boston: Allyn and Bacon.

Gold, Y. (1996). "Beginning Teacher Support: Attrition, Mentoring and Induction." In J. Sikula, T.J. Buttery, and E. Guyton (eds.), *Handbook of Research on Teacher Education.* New York: Macmillan.

Gregorian, Vartan. (2001). Op Ed Article, *New York Times,* July 9, 2001.

Gross, S. (1999). *Elementary Science in Montgomery County Maryland: A Comprehensive Transformation of a System Wide Screener Program.* ESI 91-53827. Maryland: Montgomery County Public Schools.

Hanushek, E. A., Kain, J. F., O'Brien, D. M; & Rivkin, S. G. "Good Teachers Raise Student Achievement." NBER (National Bureau of Economic Research) Working Paper No. 11154. February 2005. Retrieved from http://www.nber.org/digest/aug05/w11154.html.

Harrison, A.F. and Bramson, R. M. (1982). *The Art of Thinking.* New York: Berkeley Books.

Henderson, A. & Mapp, K. (2002). *A New Wave of Evidence: The impact of school, family and community connections on student achievement.* Austin, Texas, Southwest Educational Development Laboratory.

Hersey, P., Blanchard, K. H., and Johnson, D. E. (2000). *Management of Organizational Behavior: Leading Human Resources.* New Jersey: Prentice Hall.

Hord, S. M. (1997). "Professional Learning Communities: What are they and why are they important?" Issues about Change, Volume 6, No. 1. Austin, TX: Southwest Educational Development Laboratory.

Huling-Austin. L. (1990). "Teacher Induction Programs and Internships." In R. W. Houston (ed.), *Handbook of Research on Teacher Education.* New York: Macmillan.

Ingersoll, R. (2001). Teacher turnover and teacher shortage: An organizational analysis. *American Educational Research Journal,* 38(3).

Lambert, L. (2003). *Leadership Capacity for Lasting School Improvement.* Alexandria, VA: Association for Supervision and Curriculum Development.

Little, J. W. (1982). "Norms of Collegiality and Experimentation: Workplace Conditions of School Success." *Education Research Journal,* 19(3), 325-340.

Little, J. W. (1993). "Teachers' Professional Development in a Climate of Educational Reform." *Educational Evaluation and Policy Analysis,* 15(2), 129-151.

Marzano, R. J., Pickering, D. J., & Pollock, J. E. (2001). *Classroom Instruction that Works: Research-based strategies for increasing student achievement.* Alexandria, VA: Association for Supervision and Curriculum Development.

Ma, L. (1999). *Knowing and Teaching Elementary Mathematics: Teachers' Understanding of Fundamental Mathematics in China and the United States.* New Jersey: Lawrence Erlbaum Associates.

National Association of State Boards of Education. (1998). *The Numbers Game: Ensuring Quantity and Quality in the Teaching Work Force.* Alexandria, VA: Author.

Newmann, F. and Wehlage, F. (1999). *Successful School Restructuring.* Wisconsin: University of Wisconsin Press.

Odell, S. J. (1986). "Induction Support of New Teachers: A Fundamental Approach." *Journal of Teacher Education,* 37(1), 26-29.

Odell, S. J. and Ferraro, D. P. (1992). "Teacher Mentoring and Teacher Retention." *Journal of Teacher Education,* 43(3): 201-204.

Platt, A., et al. (1999). *The Skillful Leader: Confronting Mediocre Teaching.* Acton, MA: Author.

Rosenholtz, S. J. (1989). *Teachers' Workplace: The Social Organization of Schools.* New York: Longman.

Sanders, W.L. and Reeves, J.C. (1998). "Cumulative and Residual Effects of Teachers on Future Student Academic Achievement." In *Thinking K-16: Good Teaching Matters. How Well Qualified Teachers Can Close the Gap.* Education Trust.

Saphier, J. (1980). *The Parameters of Teaching: An Empirical Study Using Observations and Interviews to Validate a Theory of Teaching by Linking Levels of Analysis, Levels of Knowing, and Levels of Performance.* Doctoral Dissertation: Boston University.

Saphier, J. (1993). *How to Make Supervision and Evaluation Really Work.* Carlisle, MA: Research for Better Teaching.

Saphier, J. and Gower, R. (1997) *The Skillful Teacher.* Carlisle, MA: Research for Better Teaching.

Scherer, M. (Ed.). (1999). *A Better Beginning.* Alexandria, VA: Association for Supervision and Curriculum Development.

Shulman, L. (1986). "Those Who Understand: Knowledge Growth in Teaching." *Educational Researcher,* 15(2), 4-14.

Stigler, J. W. and Hiebert, J. (1988). *The Learning Gap.* New York: Summit Books.

Smith, R.M. & Ingersoll, R. M (2004). What are the effects of induction and mentoring on beginning teacher turnover? *American Educational Research Journal.* 41(3).

Sweeney, B. A. (1998). "A Survey of the 50 State-Mandated Novice Teacher Programs: Implications for State and Local Mentoring Programs and Practices." Retrieved from www.teachermentors.com

"Who Should Teach?" (January 12, 2000). *Educational Leadership.* Alexandria, VA: Association for Supervision and Curriculum Development.

Wiggins, G. and McTighe, J. (1998). *Understanding by Design.* Alexandria, VA: Association for Supervision and Curriculum Development.

Wong, H. K. (August 8, 2001). "Mentoring Can't Do It All: New Teachers Learn Best from Systematic Induction Programs." *Education Week.* Retrieved from www.newteacher.com

WEB SITES FOR NEW EDUCATORS

A Homepage for New English/Language Arts Teachers
www.ncte.org
This site offers a variety of resources and a free subscription to new language arts teachers.

A Homepage for New (And Not So New) Math Teachers
www.people.clarityconnect.com/webpages/terri/terri.html
This site is filled with ideas for new (and not so new) math teachers and includes math problems for students, internet guidelines, resources, and professional suggestions.

Science Teacher's Tool Box
www.sciencespot.net/index.html
An award winning site for science teachers and other teachers that provides a broad variety of student and teacher oriented resources for strengthening the teaching of science.

Sites for Teachers
www.sitesforteachers.com
A link to hundreds of sites for teachers, ranked by popularity.

Teachers Helping Teachers
www.pacificnet.net/~mandel

This site, 10 years old, offers basic tips for beginning teachers. It is a curriculum resource for lesson plans and has links to education sites, organized by subject and topic.

The Ultimate Teacher's Resource
www.teachers.net

This site offers lesson plans, a newsletter, and a bookshelf of resources.

What To Expect In Your First Year Of Teaching
www.ed.gov/pubs/FirstYear

This site offers suggestions and support through vignettes of new teachers in real situations.

INDEX

administrators
    professional learning communities and, 53-54
    roles in community outreach, 63-64
    roles in confidentiality, 44-45
    roles in induction program planning process, 25, 31, 35-36, 41-42
    roles in induction programs, 20, 26, 65-66
    roles in matching, 42-44, 55-58
    roles in new teacher interview process, 54-55, 67
    roles in supporting, supervising and evaluating new teachers, 69-76
    training for, 119
application process, for mentors, 36, 38-40, 122-126
assessment
    beginning teachers and, 74-76
    induction programs and, 77-80, 120
    qualitative measures, 79-80, 120
    quantitative measures, 78-79, 120
    self-assessment tool for districts, 133-135

beginning teachers
    beginning teacher network, 61-62
    belief systems, 52-53
    classroom management, 52
    confidentiality, 44-45, 84
    hiring process, 55-58, 67
    mentor pairing, 42-44, 55
    orientation, 56-58
    planning skills, 51
    roles in induction planning process, 32
    second and third year teachers, 62-63
    supervision, 74-76

mentor training

> advocacy, 52
>
> classroom management, 52
>
> communication styles, 48
>
> "differential conferencing," 50
>
> influencing beginning teachers' beliefs, 52-53
>
> lesson planning skills for beginning teachers, 51, 61
>
> model for training, 49
>
> monthly planning for beginning teachers, 52
>
> working with administrators, 53-54

"no fault bail out," 44

principals

> hiring and the interview, 54-55, 67
>
> roles in beginning teacher orientation, 57-58
>
> roles in class placement and scheduling, 68-70
>
> roles in confidentiality, 44-45, 84
>
> roles in induction planning process, 32
>
> roles in matching mentors and beginning teachers, 38-40
>
> roles in supervision, 74-76
>
> whole school engagement in the induction program, 68-73

professional learning communities

> comprehensive induction and, 19-20, 24, 53, 90-91
>
> cultural norms of, 154-155

school board/committee

> budgets for induction program, 64
>
> communication with, 63-64
>
> policy for induction program, 64
>
> roles in induction program planning, 31, 37

"sock hop" approach to matching, 43

superintendents

> role in induction planning process, 31

supervision of beginning teachers, 74-76

ABOUT *TEACHERS*[21] AND THE AUTHORS

Jon Saphier

Jon Saphier is the Founder and Chairman Emeritus of the Board of *Teachers*[21], a non-profit organization dedicated to strengthening teaching as a profession. Jon is also the Founder and President of Research for Better Teaching, a former classroom teacher, and a nationally respected staff developer and consultant. Dr. Saphier is the author of six books, including *The Skillful Teacher*, and numerous articles on staff development, supervision and evaluation, and school culture.

Susan Freedman

Susan Freedman is the President of *Teachers*[21] and co-founder of the Beginning Teacher Center of *Teachers*[21] and Simmons College. She is a former senior manager of the Educator Quality Division of the Massachusetts Department of Education, a former member of the National Commission on Families, Communities, Schools, and Children's Learning, and a former public school teacher. Susan is a former educational consultant working with districts across the country and the author and co-author of numerous publications on school restructuring and school improvement.

Barbara Aschheim

Barbara Aschheim, the former Vice-President of *Teachers*[21], has been a public school teacher, a higher education administrator, and an associate at the Massachusetts Department of Education. She is a staff developer who has worked with teachers and administrators in over 120 school districts on developing and implementing comprehensive induction programs for new teachers. Barbara is the co-author of numerous publications and articles on school-community partnerships and school improvement.

About TEACHERS[21]

Teachers[21] is a national non-profit organization dedicated to systemic education reform. Our vision is that all students will have knowledgeable educators who believe in them and who work in schools with strong cultures of professional practice. Jon Saphier and Susan Freedman, who are the founder and the president of *Teachers*[21] respectively, created the foundation on which our work is based.

Teachers[21] is reshaping the profession of teaching and school leadership through four major programmatic areas:

Professional Development

Since 1993, *Teachers*[21] has built a reputation as a key provider of knowledge-based professional development to educators nationally and across New England, including over 50% of the districts in Massachusetts.

Research, Program Development, and Dissemination

Teachers[21] develops and disseminates new knowledge that advances PreK-12 teaching and learning through its innovative programs:

- *Leadership Licensure Program*: Developed in partnership with the Massachusetts Secondary School Administrators' Association and the Massachusetts Association for Supervision and Curriculum Development, this rigorous, comprehensive state-approved program is preparing its sixth and seventh cohorts of aspiring principals for successful administrative leadership.
- *Beginning Teacher Center*: Co-founded with Simmons College in 1999, this center provides a comprehensive induction model that is creating a seamless continuum of professional support for teachers from their pre-service training throughout their first three years of teaching.
- *Urban District Improvement Model*: Based on ten change actions for systemic reform, this replicable district-wide improvement model is now finishing its fourth year of implementation in partnership with the city of Malden, which is one of the most diverse school districts in Massachusetts.

continued...

continued from previous page...

- *High School Reform*: *Teachers*[21] implements its unique model of secondary school re-design to help school districts improve the educational experiences available to their high school students and ensure that students are equipped with the skills and knowledge needed to live productive, meaningful lives after graduation.

- *The Teachers*[21] *Model of Leadership Coaching*: Based on decades of work in leadership development and systemic reform, this flexible model expands district-wide leadership capacity to support large-scale improvements in teaching and learning. The model is an integration of the knowledge bases on effective teaching, learning, and leadership. It provides a generic framework to support education leaders at all levels and to align with a district's improvement agenda. *Teachers*[21] is implementing, researching, and refining its coaching model in a number of Massachusetts school districts.

- Publications: The *Teachers*[21] publications promote emerging trends and cutting-edge thinking that advance the knowledge bases of professional practice.

Public Discourse

Teachers[21] improves public understanding about the significance and complexities of knowledge-based teaching and administration in schools by informing legislators, policymakers, opinion shapers, and business and community leaders.

Policy

Teachers[21] influences policymakers to align the ten personnel processes that impact teacher and administrator quality. At the state level, we work with legislators and staff, K-16 practitioners, and the business community to generate legislative proposals that will improve educator quality for all children in Massachusetts Public Schools. Our educator quality platform is represented in its entirety in *House 4157, An Act Relative to Teacher and Administrator Quality across Massachusetts*, which has been filed by the assistant house majority leader. At the national level, *Teachers*[21] partners with organizations such as The National Commission on Teaching and America's Future and The National Board for Professional Teaching Standards to influence discussions about policy and practice relating to educator quality.